Leaky Bucket of Profits

Plug the Holes That Drain Your Business of Cash,
Profits & Your Happiness

Tony Malyk

Tellwell Talent
www.tellwell.ca

ISBN
978-0-2288-1575-4 (Hardcover)
978-0-2288-1574-7 (Paperback)
978-0-2288-1576-1 (eBook)

Table of Contents

Endorsements

"*Leaky Bucket of Profits* is a must-read for anyone desiring time and financial freedom from their business. Tony's "Nuggets" of sage business advice will inspire and motivate you to make effectual changes in your company by giving you the tools and knowledge to improve your leadership and management skills, increase profits and generate positive cashflow. An excellent book and highly recommended."

Larry Clay, 2nd Vice President of the National Canadian Home Builders Association / President of Clay Construction Inc.

"Having known and worked with Tony for nearly a decade, the "stuff" covered in this book has proven over and over again to be the "magic" to a successful business and has been instrumental in my company being recognized by Profit 500 as one of Canada's Faster Growing companies for four consecutive years. It is concise and written in plain language with relevant anecdotal stories, so that even the busiest of us will take the time to read it."

Rod Wainwright, President, Lantrax Logistics Ltd.

"*Leaky Bucket of Profits* is an easy read with a logical and common-sense approach that uses real life business examples to enhance certain topics while laying out a methodical process to business strategy and success."

Paul Coltura, CPA, CA Partner BDO Canada LLP

"Using compelling stories and his vast knowledge, Tony Malyk's *Leaky Buckets of Profits* guides small business owners from rags to riches! I wish I would have read this 30 years ago!"

Dave Fuller Author of the book *Profit Yourself Healthy*

"If your business is stuck in a rut and you are severely overworked and barely making a living then *Leaky Bucket of Profits* is a great place to start. Tony uses real world stories from different industries to help the struggling business owner make a plan to succeed. Tony's experience helping businesses to thrive is apparent as you go through this guide to help your company plug the holes that drain your profits."

Travis Strain, Certified Financial Planner.

Acknowledgements

I started writing this book about five years ago but didn't realize it at the time. I had learned many valuable lessons and a developed a deep understanding of the challenges faced by many business owners in a variety of industries through my many meetings with them. Anxious to share this knowledge with the business community, I approached a couple local business publications about my idea to share my insights. I received an immediate response and invitation from the editor of the *Surrey Business News* in Surrey, British Columbia to send a sample article. The rest as they say is history. I wrote over twenty articles over five years for the *Surrey Business News* as well as posting numerous articles for *LinkedIn Pulse* and blogs for my own business coaching website.

Many people commented that I had already written a book with all my writing and content. I appreciated the compliments, but would respond with "well, maybe one day", with no real intention of following through with it. My mind changed in 2016 while attending a business coaching conference with the *Professional Business Coaches Alliance (PBCA)*. A fellow business coach, Dave Fuller, had just published his own book, *Profit Yourself Healthy*, and encouraged me to use my writing portfolio to write my own book. It was at that moment that writing a book seemed possible. I had a couple false starts as I struggled with how to pull it all together. I used my business coach training on myself to determine what was my first step was to get started. I decided to write the introduction to frame the book and my book writing journey began in November 2018.

There are many people I need to thank who encouraged and supported me before and during my book writing journey. Thank you, Rod Wainwright for your trust and confidence over the years and for acting as my editor so this book wouldn't be filled with typos. Thank you, Patricia Lessard for your encouragement and support as we entered the world of entrepreneurship together and for your feedback to make this book more expressive.

I would like to thank Jim Shopland, Beverley Rosin and Bruce Styles of my LeaderImpact group for your support, encouragement and prayers. God bless!

My brother Andy had a profound impact on this book, before and during the writing process. He called me out when I deserved it, listened to me during my failures and joined me as I celebrated my successes. He gave me honest feedback on this book and provided valuable insights based on his own professional career. Thank you, bunjauch.

A big part of my motivation for writing this book was to leave a legacy that my family could be proud of. Whenever I felt myself running out of energy I would think of my children, Stefan and Taryne and their spouses, Natalie and Tom. I would think of my grandchildren, Annika, Logan, Oliver, Karra and Nova. I would think of my wife, Diane. She has supported me and stood by me every time I changed jobs or careers which at times created a lot of uncertainty about our future. Looking back, it is these collective experiences that became the foundation for this book. You have all blessed my life and given me purpose.

To my late parents, Tony (Tommy) and Elizabeth Malyk and my extended family. You all instilled blue-collar values in me of hard work, honesty, integrity and pride that shaped my outlook and beliefs. It kept me grounded and I never forgot where I came from. Thank you to my aunts and uncles: Bob & Anne Malyk, Vic & Jean Malyk, Bill & Anne Yurkiw, Bill & Kay Babinchuk, Nick & Nellie Horosko, Bud & Mary Evans and Harold & Kay Trybel. Thank you to my grandparents (Gigi & Baba), Bill & Mary Malyk and Andrew Mostoway.

Finally, this book would not have been possible without the over one hundred business owners who agreed to either meet with me or trusted me to be their business coach. As much as I did my best to provide you value, you returned the value to me many times over by sharing your challenges, frustrations and insights, many of which inspired the content of this book. I wrote this book for you.

Introduction

While growing up in Manitoba, Canada, my brother and I spent parts of many summers and weekends on our grandparent's farm. We had several chores to do while there but one that I remember the most is feeding the pigs. We used an old rusty galvanized metal bucket that leaked due to the numerous holes developed after many years of use. We pumped water from the well by hand as fast as we could into the old rusty bucket so it would fill faster than the water exiting through the various leaks. We would then run as fast as we could to the pig trough to fill it with whatever water that had not already leaked out.

The memory of working feverously so that the water would enter the bucket quicker than the pace of water exiting the bucket never left me as I progressed through my management and business coaching careers. I have met over one hundred frustrated business owner who thought that more sales would solve their problems with cash flow, profits and general stress.

After analyzing many businesses, I found that sales were often not the problem like many business owners thought. There was in fact, adequate sales to be a profitable, cash positive business. The issue was the business was a leaky bucket of profits. Think of water as money as it enters the bucket as sales. There is a spigot at the bottom that is always partially open drawing water from your bucket representing usual expenses. If water enters the bucket faster than the spigot releases it the bucket starts to overflow creating the need for a bigger bucket. This a good since it means you need to expand your business to hold all the extra water.

However, if the spigot is open too much or you have holes in your bucket you will need to add water faster to keep up with the discharge. In other words, you need to increase sales just to keep up with the money exiting your business. Imagine how quickly and how much your bucket would overflow with cash if you plugged the profit holes while maintaining the same level of sales and were able to do so while working less. How would this change your life today and tomorrow, not to mention your stress level?

Although you will gain some knowledge on how to increase sales in this book the primary goal will be for you to learn how to recognize and plug the holes that are draining your business of cash, profits and your happiness. When I started writing this book my intention was to focus on the "Magic Profit Formula" and "Manage Like a CEO" sections with just a small part of the book dedicated to leadership. As I continued writing and remembering the many meetings I had with business owners, it became very apparent that most struggle with leadership which was the root cause of many underperforming businesses. With this revelation in mind I rewrote the section, "It Starts with You", to deepen the discussion on leadership and provide insights that many seem to lack. The result is that this section is now three times the size of the original version.

In Section 1, *It starts With You,* we start with talking about you. As a business owner, it is crucial that you are the best leader possible because as mentioned above, ineffective leadership is the root of what ails most businesses and can have a profound effect on profitability. Companies that are not effectively lead tend to have confused and unmotivated employees. All of this results in low productivity, low profits, poor cash flow and ongoing stress. This book will share key leadership principles of how to get your company focused and help you develop your own vision and core values. We will then talk about how to motivate your employees, so they are ready and willing to step up to help you achieve your vision. You will learn to understand communication styles so you can communicate more effectively with your team and create a more harmonious environment.

In Section 2, *The Magic Profit Formula,* you will learn a proven process in detail, on how to recognize the profit holes in your business and to develop strategies to plug those profit holes and generate profitable growth. You will be shown how to review all areas of your business and to develop strategies to improve performance in each area including sales & marketing, customer service, operations, human resources and finance and administration.

In Section 3, *Manage Like a CEO,* you will learn about the same management tools that CEOs use to track and manage their business, so you can run your business as well as "the big guys". Key topics such as how to track performance, cash flow management and financial management are covered. You will also gain valuable knowledge on how to structure your business to maximize your business's value while achieving the work/life balance you and your family deserve.

I grew up in a blue-collar household with blue-collar neighbors and was surrounded by an extended blue-collar family. Hard work, honesty, faith and heritage was our foundation. I spent my career learning how to run businesses in blue-collar industries. I have learned lessons from my successes, I have learned lessons from my failures, and I learned an immense amount from the many business owners I have either met or served as a business coach. They have shared their struggles, fears and challenges with me, and I am honored and thrilled to share my lessons learned with you so you can fast track your own success. I wrote this book for you, the hard-working blue-collar business owner who deserves more, just like my family.

Let's get to work!

Section I

It Starts with You

Chapter 1

Build a Winning Culture

I know it sounds mushy, but it works!

Let's recognize that good or bad, you and only you put your business into the situation that it is in right now. If your sales are stagnating or diminishing it is because you ineffectively marketed or failed to develop your product so that it is appealing to your customers. If you are challenged by poor cash flow or profitability it is because you failed to implement fundamental controls to track and manage key factors effectively. If you are frustrated by unmotivated employees who constantly make mistakes or have low productivity it is because you have been ineffective in leading and motivating them.

In his book, *The E-Myth Revisited,* Michael Gerber makes it very clear that a business is a direct reflection of the owner. He says, "if your thinking is sloppy, your business will be sloppy". "If you are greedy, your employees will be greedy", so if you want your business to change then you must change first. In other words, if you want a better, more successful business, It Starts with You!

Assembling a highly competent, motivated and focused team is the most important step a leader makes when building a successful business. The best strategies and tactics in the world used to improve business performance will fail without the support of the team. Despite this, many business owners either neglect or fail miserably with leadership. Having strong processes and systems in place with a weak and unmotivated team to run them will cause unlimited stress for the business owner as he spends endless hours fighting fires and correcting his staff's mistakes. However, a business with weak systems can still achieve acceptable results due to the resolve of a motivated team working to overcome the shortcomings of a weak system.

I met with an electrical contractor with twenty employees where the owner spent most of his day fielding phone calls and solving everyone's problems. By the end of his fourteen-hour day he was exhausted, frustrated and when all was said and done, he struggled to make payroll. He constantly worried about the impact his business would have on his family's future. As we conducted a business review it became apparent that he had unintentionally built a culture based on the premise, "don't move until the boss approves it." There were some systems in place, but the owner had a reputation of "blowing up" on staff when they made a mistake. No one wanted to take responsibility for their own actions, so they always defaulted to the boss resulting in him spending most of his time fielding phone calls and fighting fires. He felt like he was running an adult daycare but soon realized that his behavior and actions was the primary driver of his company's culture. If the culture was to change, he needed to change. We will talk more about this in *Chapter 2, Be a Dynamic Leader*.

The Meaning of Company Culture

I attended an event where the keynote speaker was a local business owner of a prominent window manufacturing and renovation company with over 150 employees. As he spoke about the culture of his company, he explained how he sought out employees at all levels, who were competitive, entrepreneurial, sports minded, had strong personal values and demonstrated a genuine desire to give back to the community. He went on to explain how he would replace any employee who lost their "edge". It was a "work hard, play hard" environment. He demanded that employees always keep their hunger alive and to never stop finding ways to improve themselves and the company.

At first, I thought, "where does this all come from?" It didn't take long to realize that this businessman possessed all the above attributes he had just described. He was intense and unforgiving, yet he was empathetic and dedicated to the success of everyone of his employees. The culture of his company was a direct reflection of his personality and values. His business thrived because he was able to clearly describe with every detail, what his company stood for and wouldn't accept anything less. He never lowered his standards so others could just fit in. Some people flourished in his environment, achieving amazing results while others struggled and left. As the leader it is imperative that you drive your company's culture or it will drive you.

When asked, most employees are not able to define the culture of the company they work for. Culture is not defined just by the written word but a combination of the "intangibles" that drive how people will act and react in their environment. A company's culture can be based on passion and excellence like the one described above, or it can be based on characteristics such as control, intimidation, fear, political correctness, politeness, mutual respect or to "not rock the boat", just to name a few.

How many business owners or CEOs can truly describe the culture of their company and back it up with real life examples of how the actions of their management team, employees and even themselves drive the culture they describe?

The "Circle of Safety"

In his book, *Leaders Eat Last,* Simon Sinek talks about the importance of having a "circle of safety" in an organization. He uses the U.S. Marines as an example of an organization whose existence and survival are dependent on a deeply rooted culture built on trust. During their training, marines are put through numerous challenges and tests. Some of their training focuses on the technical skills marines need to perform their duties but more importantly, the primary focus is to shape their mindset and to weed out those that don't belong. They are conditioned to always have their colleagues backs no matter what, and in return they can expect to trust their colleagues with their lives. Everything they do and think is based on contributing to the team's success. With an untouchable level of mutual trust team members can move forward with complete confidence because they don't have to keep looking over their shoulder. Those who do not meet the extremely high standard of character to be in the circle of trust are not allowed in even if they have exceptional technical skills. Those who break or threaten the circle are immediately removed. The "circle" is sacred and is everyone's responsibility to guard and protect it.

I reviewed two auto service centers each with similar sales and about seven employees. In one case the owner showed trust and confidence in his team. The workplace was organized and clean, it has the most up to date equipment and the staff had confidence knowing that the owner had their back. They rarely made a mistake but when they did make a mistake it was treated as a "learning opportunity" so it wouldn't happened again. The second service center was completely opposite. Although it also had state of the art equipment, the workplace was disorganized and dirty and mistakes were constantly being made by technicians. Instead of treating mistakes as learning opportunities the owner would literally yell and scream at his staff, belittling them in the process. They had little confidence, and an apathetic attitude for their job, their boss and teammates. There was no safety in the circle. The difference in employee turnover and business performance was staggering. The second business turned over his whole staff a full two times (200%) per year and sustained losses of over $50,000 per year. It eventually went out of business. The first business had very little turnover with an employee leaving every two years or so not to mention it made six figure profits every year. So here you have it, two similar sized businesses where one struggles while the other flourishes. What is the difference? It came down to leadership and company culture.

As you can see by the above example, it's not just the leader's words that drive the culture it is also their actions. A leader whose actions are not congruent with their message can create a culture of distrust or confusion. It is imperative that the leader remains passionate about the culture of their company and constantly ensures that management and employees are supporting the culture the leader desires for their organization.

The foundation to developing a strong company culture is having a clearly stated Vision, Mission and Values statements. You have probably heard this before and I know that it all sounds touch feely and mushy, but the fact is that it works and is foundational to a successful business. These become the guiding light for staff and management when making tough decisions and gives direction on how they should conduct themselves. More importantly, it can turn companies into high performing organizations, attracting the "right" people who are very clear of their vision and what they need to achieve every day.

Core Values

The *core values* of your organization should not be manufactured to sound good to others. For them to be authentic, core values should come from your heart. They should be personal and unwavering even in the most trying times and requiring the most difficult decisions. Whenever you find yourself deciding on strategy or on how to handle an immediate difficult situation your first test should be to ask yourself, "does this fit with my core values". If the answer is "yes", then proceed. If the answer is "no", reconsider your decision. You can't expect your team to honor and live up to your core values if you don't do so yourself.

I met the owner of a plumbing business who proudly told me that one of his company's core values was honesty. A few months after making this proud comment we uncovered a situation where he authorized an employee to replace an expensive part that didn't really need to be replaced. When confronted with this his responded with a laugh and said, "it would have to be replaced someday anyway". Think of the message he was giving to his employee. His words said "honesty", but his actions said otherwise.

In contrast to the above, here is an example of a company that was unwavering in living by its core values. One of the core values of a distribution company was "customer is king" and its leadership lived it every day. When a customer needed something quickly it was couriered overnight at no extra charge. If a customer returned a product claiming to be faulty it was accepted even when the customer service person knew it wasn't faulty. Employees who did not live by the "customer is king" value were either reprimanded or fired. This created a strong culture that sprung the company to the top of its industry.

Fig 1.1

Integrity	Honesty	Excellence	Hard Working
Respect	Generosity	Innovative	Customer Focused
Proactive	Community	Reliability	Consistent
Efficient	Passion	Education	Diversity
Team Work	Quality	Empathy	Collaborative
Accountable	Opportunity	Open Minded	Sustainability
Giving	Humility	Fun	Entrepreneurial

To develop your own list of cores values, review the sample list in *Fig1.1*. Feel free to add words that you don't see that should be there. Next, develop a short list of 10 – 12 words by circling the ones that feels the most right to you. They should make you feel warm and fuzzy in side. Now, pare those words down even further to a final list of five core values that you will not waver from. Here is an interesting question, are you already living by these core values or are you still aspiring to live by them? If your answer is the latter, then ask yourself what actions do you need to start taking right now so you are living by your core values? Don't worry if you can't answer this question right now. It will be covered in more detail in the next chapter.

Vision Statement

Like core values, the vision statement is also inspirational, capturing the imagination of those both inside and outside the organization. It usually has three to five words that describes the long-term impact that you want your organization to have on your industry, your community or even the world. It becomes the purpose of your organization and the cause that your team will rally around.

Think about why you started or bought your business. Was it to just simply make money or did you want to have an impact on your industry, community or even society? When you think of your vision statement it should inspire you and those around you. Simply put, it is an ideological statement of something that hasn't happened yet but if you are successful it would be achieved in the long term.

We have all heard thought-provoking statements from well-known visionaries about their view of the future world. Microsoft's vision in its early days was "a computer on every desk and in every home". This clearly stated that Microsoft wanted to make computers available to everyday people, so that people could learn and connect around the world. With this vision clearly communicated, every employee of Microsoft was focused on designing and producing software that would make computers easy for the average person to use and at a price they could afford.

In contrast, Steve Jobs', the founder of Apple Computers, original vision for Apple was to build "computers for the rest of us" which at the time offered an alternative choice to those who didn't want to follow the masses but wanted to challenge the "establishment". They focused not only being better that Microsoft at everything they did but being different as well. They became the anti-Microsoft, building a strong following of loyal customers that bought into their protest like movement.

Mission Statement

The *Mission Statement* is a sentence or in some cases a few sentences depending on the organization, that clearly communicates the big picture of how your company will achieve its vision. Whereas a Vision Statement describes an outcome the Mission Statement is an action statement. A well-constructed Mission statement should not be manufactured to just sound good, it should come from the heart and include information about "who you are", "what you do" and "who you do it for". If done correctly your team will understand what actions, it needs to focus on every single day so the organization can achieve its vision. Here are some examples of mission statements from some of the world's best-known game changing companies.

"To be Earth's most customer-centric company, where customers can find and discover anything they might want to buy online, and endeavors to offer its customers the lowest possible prices." Amazon.com

"To enable people and businesses throughout the world to realize their full potential." Microsoft

"Uber is evolving the way the world moves. By seamlessly connecting riders to drivers through our apps, we make cities more accessible, opening up more possibilities for riders and more business for drivers." UBER

Fig 1.2

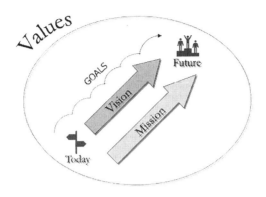

The Absolute Power of Clarity

I was rejoicing in a client's new-found success when I remembered a conversation, I had with a Business Coach years before becoming a Business Coach myself. I asked him what exactly a Business Coach does, and his reply was, "I help my clients get **clarity**".

The look on my face must have shocked him as my jaw dropped. I didn't say it out loud, but I couldn't believe that people would pay someone a significant amount of money just to get "clarity". What was the value in that!

At the time of this conversation I had no idea that I would become a Business Coach myself just a few years later. But now, after working with many business owners I truly understand the value in having "clarity".

With the power of *clarity* to propel them, I have watched as numerous clients doubled their business, increase their profits by hundreds of thousands of dollars and built a level of net worth in their business that they had never dreamed before.

So, what exactly is clarity and what makes it so powerful? Clarity is a point of consciousness where an individual knows exactly <u>what</u> they are trying to achieve, they know exactly <u>why</u> they are doing it and exactly <u>how</u> they are going to achieve it. They wake up every day with a deep sense of purpose and know the exact actions they must complete to achieve their goals and fulfill their purpose and vision. There is no longer confusion or indecisiveness of how to spend their time. They move forward with complete conviction.

Now imagine the power of an organization when everyone has complete clarity in their roles. They show up to work with conviction and purpose. They know exactly what they need to do to help the organization reach its goals. The level of power truly becomes greater than the sum of its parts and reaches a level of sustainability that takes on a life of its own. In the case of the client I mentioned earlier, their sales doubled, and profits quadrupled in less than four years because the productivity of every employee increased dramatically from knowing what activities they needed to spend their time on to get the best results.

So before you complete one more task sit back and ask yourself, "Do I have true clarity in what I want, why am I doing and how I am going to do it" then ask yourself, "does my staff have truly clarity in what, why and how they are going to help the company achieve its goals.

If you can answer even a remote "yes" to either of the above questions then congratulations, you are in the minority. If your answer is "no" like most, then stop what you are doing right now and invest in finding your clarity. It will pay off like you never imagined.

Cupcakes and Company Culture

Cupcakes have been around for decades but their recent rise in popularity is signaling a shift in society and corporate culture. It wasn't very long ago that a cake was the staple for celebrations. In our personal lives we all shared a cake at birthdays, weddings or other milestones. At work it may have been landing a big account, reaching a goal or any other business success.

When we share part of a cake, we are part of a bigger whole, something bigger than us. Every piece of cake is a little different from one another just like we are, but it is still part of something bigger. There is a sense of community that comes from sharing a cake that brings us all together.

The cultural shift has been from being happy to be part of something special to a focus on individuality. Cupcakes do not come from a bigger whole. They are individually wrapped and decorated and are even baked in their own compartments. We don't share cupcakes, we choose the one we want, unwrap it and eat it without it ever really being part of a bigger whole.

We can see evidence of the individualistic mindset in all parts of society and corporate culture. Technology allows us to customize our experience everywhere we go. We can set the internet browser on our computer to look and contain the exact content we want, companies can tailor the content that is sent to us based on our interests and we can choose the exact ingredients to have on our sub sandwich or in our coffee. It is no longer enough to have the choice of ordering a coffee with milk and/or sugar. Now we can order our coffee with low fat, high fat, extra hot, with multiple pumps of this and that all so we can have a coffee that is unique only to us.

In many cases employees are more focused on achieving their own personal goals and agenda over achieving company goals. Their demand for work/life balance has created an expectation that companies should accommodate their agenda vs the employee making the adjustments to accommodate the team's agenda. Unless the employee and organization can find their common ground, the result is often disengaged employees and very little loyalty.

Changing a culture is a process that involves small incremental changes over time. If you find an individualistic mindset has taken over your corporate culture, there are actions you can take to change your culture to a more team-oriented mindset. Firstly, it starts with you. As the leader it is imperative that you set the example. You are constantly under a microscope where your teammates are watching for congruency between every one of your words and actions. If your actions show that it's all about you and not the team, they will follow suit. Even a small disconnect will be very apparent to your team.

If your tradition has been to serve cupcakes at company celebrations trying serving cake and explain the change. It will be the start of a more positive mindset that will serve your organization very well.

Here are a few tips to help change your company's culture:

1. Understand your own personality. Trying to drive a culture that doesn't fit your personality and values will be uncomfortable and will be hard to maintain a high level of energy for an extended period. Your team will very aware if you are ingenuine.
2. Hire people who will fit your company's culture. Just like yourself it will be difficult for them to be consistent with your culture in the long run if it is not natural to them. Understand their values and their attitude towards their work. Take your time and build a number of steps into your hiring process to fully vet the candidate. Remember these two mantras, "'hire for attitude and train for skill" and "hire slow, fire fast". No matter their level of skill, team members who are determined to work against your company's culture should be removed immediately. Nobody is bigger than the team.
3. Live it! Breath it! Act It! Your team will always be watching you to get their cue on how to act or react daily.

The best way to ensure that the culture you desire is fully entrenched in your organization is to watch and listen to your front-line employees. If they are not living the culture you desire it could be a sign that someone in your company hierarchy is diluting your culture with behaviors that are not consistent with yours. If the front-line employees that are not living by your desired culture report directly to you then your actions and communication may not be congruent with your intentions. Your company reflects you. Are you happy with it? If not, you just might have a leadership issue.

Chapter 2

Be a Dynamic Leader

A look in the mirror

The 3 Stages of Leadership

The success or failure of an organization is determined by the effectiveness of its leader. Effective leaders are so invaluable that many organizations such as companies and sport teams happily pay millions of dollars to attract CEOs, Coaches and General Managers. We often see team members acknowledge their coach and management when they win a championship. On the other hand, how many times have ineffective leaders been blamed for the failure of their organization? It is normal to expect a certain number of coaches and general managers to be fired during a sports season. We know that their ultimate demise was due to poor team performance, but the underlying reason was the coach was simply ineffective in leading the team.

So how do we develop our leadership skills so that we can make our organization, community and world a better place? First, we need to recognize that there are three levels of leadership that a leader must achieve to be a truly effective leader. They are: *Lead Yourself, Lead Others* and *Lead Your Organization*. Each is a building block where a level of proficiency must be achieved at one level before one can expect to be effective at the next level.

Lead Yourself First

To be a truly effective leader you must first take care of your own back yard before leading others. Effective leaders are very well grounded and comfortable in their own skin, giving them the confidence and conviction to attract and inspire others to work toward a common goal with unstoppable resolve and persistence.

Becoming grounded is achieved through a blend of attributes. Grounded leaders have a high degree of self-awareness, a clear vision and mission for their own life all wrapped with unshakable core values. Self-awareness comes from acknowledging our strengths and weaknesses, knowing how to leverage our strengths while accepting our weaknesses. Leaders are aware of how and why they react to different situations and have the presence of mind to filter or control their response, so they can achieve the best possible outcome. For example, a leader who is not self-aware is more likely to lash out at a team member for making a mistake whereas a more self-aware leader who will control his emotions and respond in a more professional and caring way, understanding that the team member was trying their best and may need more training.

I have asked hundreds of people over many years what they felt were the most important qualities of a dynamic leader. Dozens of qualities have been stated but there are twelve qualities shown in *Figure 2.1* that come up more often than any other. As you read through the twelve qualities you will start to recognize some qualities in yourself or in others. You might also find yourself feeling uncomfortable as you have trouble recognizing other qualities in yourself. For example, if you are not *decisive* you can improve this by reading books, taking assessments or specific leadership training. This is all part of growing as a leader.

Dynamic leaders treat their leadership skills like a golf swing. They never stop working on them no matter how good they may already be at it. In hockey, goal scorers never stop working on their shot, passers never stop working on their passing and goalies never stop working on their technique and hand speed. President John F. Kennedy once said, "Leading and learning are indispensable to each other".

There are numerous self-assessment tools available to help you become more self-aware. Myers Briggs is well known for identifying 16 leadership styles and their attributes, Emotional Intelligence (EI) helps to understand and control our reactions to different situations, StrengthsFinder 2.0 by Tom Rath helps you identify your strengths, so you can leverage them better to improve effectiveness and DISC is a great assessment tool to help improve your communication skills in business and life. I encourage you to seek these out if you want to develop as a leader.

Lead Others

Leading others is about developing relationships with each member of your team. A dynamic leader has the rare ability to recognize a person's strengths and weaknesses and then help that person reach their potential so they can achieve amazing results. They focus on developing and building on a person's strengths while supporting and improving on their weaknesses. It is your job to understand the goals of motivations of every one of your team member's goals and motivations, so you can inspire them to achieve amazing results. Your focus must be on developing their skills so they can grow in their job, within your organization and as people. It is imperative that you understand how to communicate with each team member, so you can have the most positive outcome possible from your interaction with them whether it is to motivate them or to hold them accountable for poor performance.

Mike Babcock, a renowned NHL Head Coach with over 1200 wins to his credit with three teams including the Anaheim Ducks, Detroit Red Wings and Toronto Maple Leafs (as of the writing of this book) and championships at numerous levels including the Stanley Cup, Canadian Interuniversity Sport (CIS), IIHF World Junior and an Olympic Gold

Medal is a great example of the importance of understanding each team member to achieve outstanding results. He had the following quote during an interview with <u>Sportsnet.ca</u> on February 17, 2017.

> *"Each team you coach is different, and every person is different,*
> *so when you coach the team you have 23 different plans*
> *for 23 different players. Now, they still have to fit into the*
> *structure of the team—the team comes first—but the reality*
> *is, we want everyone to be the best they can possibly be."*

Like most coaches in sport, Babcock spends his share of time on game strategy. What separates him from many coaches is the amount of time and energy he devotes to developing relationships with each player on a human level. He understands the best way to communicate with each player to get his point across whether he is trying to motivate them or hold them accountable for poor performance. He also able to recognize a player's untapped potential and put them in situations where they can build confidence, develop their skills and achieve levels of success they never previously thought would be possible

Fig 2.1

Passionate	Visionary	Accountable
Communicator	Integrity	Humble
Consistent	Congruent	Reliable
Empathetic	Inspiring	Motivator

Communication is one of the leadership characteristics listed in *Figure 2.1* and is so important to becoming a dynamic leader that I have devoted all of Chapter 3 to it. If there is one leadership skill that if you could improve that would have a dramatic effect on your ability to manage your business, it is without a doubt, communication.

Lead Your Organization

With a strong self-awareness of your own leadership style and abilities as well as the strengths and weaknesses of your individual team members you are now ready to lead your organization. The difference is instead of leading each person on an individual basis your ability to lead and communicate on a much larger scale is crucial to your success. Communicating your organization's Mission, Vision and Values to the team must be your top priority. You must excel at rallying your team to give all their energy and commitment to achieve your vision and contribute to your organization's success

In the case of a hockey team it is possible for a head coach to lead individual team members but with a typical roster of twenty-three players even he needs help. A head coach relies on his assistant coaches and team captains to spread his message and philosophy to the team. Whether you have five, 10, 20 or 50 employees you also need help. You can't be expected to have close relationships with everyone once your business grows beyond fifteen or twenty employees. If you try to have close relationships with every employee, you will spend every waking hour spreading your message and having to deal with issues ranging from motivation to discipline. If you have a lead hand, supervisor or department manager be sure to leverage them to spread your message and create the company culture you want just as a head coach utilizes his coaching staff and captains. They are closer to the front lines of your business than you and are in a much better position to spend the time needed with each individual team member. Remember that their actions and behavior reflect you so be sure they are very clear on your expectations of them.

Whether your employees report directly to you or through your management team, there are many strategies and tools available to help you lead your organization. Some of the most common tools and strategies include regular team meetings, written strategies, digital strategies, signage and even your policies and procedures.

Team meetings can take different forms and frequency based on the purpose of the meeting and the number of people participating. I know of contractors that have a daily "tool box talk" where they will have a quick 10-minute huddle with the crew at the job site to deal with site specific issues such as schedules, safety and workmanship plus take time to reinforce the culture of the company. They always take a minute to review the core values and mission statement and reward those who displayed behavior supporting those core values and company mission. The reward can range from just singling the individual out in the meeting with special recognition or rewarding him with a coffee card or any other small gift that the crew would fine desirable. Meetings can also be held weekly, monthly or quarterly if needed usually ranging from thirty to sixty minutes for a weekly meeting to longer for less frequent meetings depending on the agenda and items that need to be covered. No matter the frequency, always take the opportunity to reinforce your company culture.

Written strategies combined with digital strategies are effective in communicating company culture. The old-fashioned company newsletter is still very relevant if you make it relevant to your employees. News about company success is fine but focusing on stories about employees and community involvement especially when the stories support your company culture is very effective. If the need to communicate is more immediate, emails and memos still work. When possible, combining written strategies with digital platforms is very efficient and effective. You could tell the same stories featured in your newsletter by posting on a company social media page such as LinkedIn, Facebook, Instagram or Twitter to name just a few where your employees can share your stories with others in their own network, increasing the profile of your business.

Consider installing signs or digital boards within your facility that can display your core values and other messaging to support your company culture. By seeing and reading your messaging everyday your message will be ingrained into your employees and will drive the behavior you desire. Be very aware that your team will be watching you with a magnifying glass to see if your actions match your words. All the money and effort you invest into driving your company culture will go to waste if your employees catch any sign of inconsistency.

Be Ready to Take Action

I was working with an HVAC contractor client who was frustrated with the performance of his business. He said that he needed to change the culture of the company. When I asked him, what needed to change he said, "accountability, my crew doesn't hand in their paper work on time and just keeps giving me excuses." I asked him who's was responsible for letting that happen and he didn't hesitate to accept responsibility. From a leadership perspective it was encouraging that he was accepting accountability for the state of his business, but he needed to take action. We developed a written policy clearly stating that all paperwork from the previous day had to be submitted to the office at 8:00 the following day. It also clearly stated that the consequence for noncompliance would be all work orders for that day would not be included in monthly production bonuses. The client, who had already started holding weekly thirty-minute tech meetings introduced the written policy. Initially the techs balked, and a couple even defied the directive and didn't hand in their paperwork on time. The culture changed quickly when the defiant techs missed their production bonus. At first, they huffed and puffed in displeasure but with a new understanding that there was a higher level of accountability in the company they eventually complied. Policies and procedures are very effective tools to help drive culture and behavior, but they only work if you are willing to enforce them.

Business owners and managers who become effective leaders are much more likely to build successful and sustainable businesses. Leading your organization comes down to three distinct steps. (1) Decide what type of culture you want in your business (2) Communicate the behaviors you expect to drive the culture (3) Don't accept behavior that is not aligned with your culture and if possible, reward those who demonstrate alignment with your culture.

Walk the Talk

Has a leader ever said to you or have you ever caught yourself saying, "do as I say not as I do"? This statement gave me one of my first experiences with leadership and it wasn't good.

During my early teens I was an army cadet in Canada. It was a great way for someone in their teens to learn about discipline, teamwork and leadership. One summer I was participating in a six-week camp that was really a boot camp for teenagers. We were taught to pay attention to minor details like being sure that our boots were so shiny you could use them as a mirror and see your reflection. We would apply copious amounts of iron spray to our pants so the creases were so sharp you could almost cut your finger on them. We all took pride in looking sharp.

One day, a cadet officer came up to me and said that my boots were not shiny enough. I looked down at his boots and noticed that they were not any shinier than mine and even less so. I broke military protocol and pointed out to him that his boots were not very shiny either. His response was, "do as I say not as I do". This left me confused, dejected and I lost complete respect for this person and started questioning authority. Did leadership mean there were two sets of rules? One for leaders and another for the rest?

As leaders we must recognize that those whom we lead have us under a microscope. They are always watching to see if our actions are matching our words. Any lack of congruency between our words and actions are magnified and will lead to apathy and distrust in our organization. Once trust is lost it takes a very long time to regain it, resulting in a downward trend of diminishing performance.

I unfortunately experienced similar situations during my corporate career where the actions of business owners, managers and even company Presidents did not reflect the values and standards they so passionately communicated. There was a distribution company that lost its signature product causing it to fall on hard times. Sales plummeted by forty per cent overnight. The company was hemorrhaging cash and needed to take drastic action. The President preached fiscal restraint as people were laid off and costs were cut where ever possible. Company executives were asked to give up their luxury company cars for much cheaper economy models. All complied except for one person, the President himself. The person who asked everyone else to sacrifice refused to do the same. His message of showing fiscal restraint fell on deaf ears as the common reaction was, "if you're not willing to sacrifice then why should I". Business performance worsened in the following months and the company was eventually sold at a dramatic discount.

Leaders who preach fiscal restraint then take lavish vacations or express appreciation for employees with many years of loyal and dedicated service then unceremoniously lay them off to save money are not demonstrating congruency between their words and actions.

Here are a few tips to help you maintain congruency between your words and actions:

1. Live by your core values every day even when it is inconvenient. If one of your core values is *honesty*, then don't ask your staff to lie to a customer when there is a missed shipment or misdiagnosis of a malfunctioning piece of equipment even if it costs you some profits to resolve the problem
2. Remember that the true character of a person is what they do when no one is watching. If one of your core values is *respect*, then treat others with respect all the time, not just when at work.

3. Don't ask anyone do to anything that you wouldn't do yourself. If you don't keep your vehicle clean and organized all the time, then don't expect you team to either.

If you truly believe and live by the words you say, you will earn the undying respect and loyalty of your team, run a more effective organization and leave a legacy that will outlast your being.

Every Manager Should Know the "Rule of the Hog"

A new manager started his first management job running a wood manufacturing plant. He wanted to make a name for himself and was determined to increase productivity and whip labour into shape.

His boss warned him that the employees "owned the Hog". The Hog is a machine used to chip unusable raw material for waste removal. The new manager didn't listen and being determined to drive the numbers started to demand that the employees work harder, made cut backs on safety programs and purchasing tools and then stopped reward programs that were meant to motivate employees because he felt they were a waste of time and money.

It didn't take long before productivity and yields from raw material plummeted along with profits. The new manager didn't understand that "owning the Hog" meant if the employees were not happy, they would throw perfectly good raw material into the chipper in spite. Eventually the new manager became a victim of the Hog and was fired.

So, what's the morale of this story? Team members will always find a way to get their pound of flesh back from the leader. If they are treated with respect and feel appreciated, they will look after your best interests and give their best effort. If not, they will find subtle ways to take back control such as taking very little care to minimize waste or giving only the minimal effort to get the job done when they could have given so much more. This will certainly drive down profits and shows in several ways including declining KPIs, quality control issues, call backs and absenteeism.

It is equally important that managers are not held hostage by labour as it is their job to find a balance between holding members accountable for poor performance while maintaining their respect and loyalty. How can a manager find this balance? Here are a few tips:

1. Get your employees involved in the decision-making process. If improvements are needed, present the problem and ask for their recommendations. They are often very happy to be part of the solution.
2. Most people know when they are not performing at an acceptable level. Rather than accusing them and demanding better performance bring it to their attention and ask why it is happening. If they deny it then calmly back up your statement with facts such as productivity reports then ask them how they will improve. Once the facts are confirmed ask them once again for their help in improving performance.
3. Be sure to show appreciation when there is improvement. Showing appreciation is a simple yet very powerful motivator.

The key is to balance respect with firmness. Team members will appreciate being held accountable if done so with respect and empathy. There are often underlying reasons why productivity and performance are lagging. A skilled manager will uncover and deal with the source of the problem rather than just deal with the symptom.

Herzberg's Two-Factor Theory

The owner of an electrical contracting company once asked me how to motivate employees. His techs and office staff did what they needed to do to get the job done but that was it. There was no extra effort or passion being displayed, no one wanted to work overtime or step up when they were needed the most. In frustration he said, "I don't know what the problem is, I pay good wages and benefits, I buy them coffee and donuts once in a while". I sat down with him and explained Herzberg's Two-Factor Theory.

Herzberg's Two-Factor Theory was developed in 1964 by psychologist Frederick Herzberg as the result of a study of 203 engineers and architects in Pittsburg. Engineers and architects were chosen due to their growing importance in society. They were asked about periods of their lives when they were happy and unhappy with their jobs. Here is the exact quote from Herzberg himself in 1964 as it appears on the website: https://en.wikipedia.org/wiki/Two-factor_theory.

> *"Briefly, we asked our respondents to describe periods in their lives when they were exceedingly happy and unhappy with their jobs. Each respondent gave as many "sequences of events" as he could that met certain criteria— including a marked change in feeling, a beginning, and an end, and contained some substantive description other than feelings and interpretations...*

> *The proposed hypothesis appears verified. The factors on the right that led to satisfaction (achievement, intrinsic interest in the work, responsibility, and advancement) are mostly unipolar; that is, they contribute very little to job dissatisfaction. Conversely, the dis-satisfiers (company policy and administrative practices, supervision, interpersonal relationships, working conditions, and salary) contribute very little to job satisfaction."*

Fig 2.2

Herzberg Two-Factor Theory

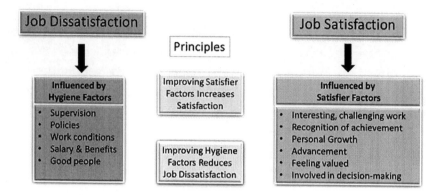

The results of the study are illustrated in *Fig 2.2*. Attributes of the workplace were divided into two types of factors: *Hygiene Factors* and *Satisfier Factors*. Hygiene factors includes salary, benefits, policies, supervision, working conditions and working with good people. Satisfier factors includes Interesting, challenging work, personal growth, recognition of achievement, opportunity for advancement, feeling valued and being involved in decision making.

The study conclude that hygiene factors are not motivators, but the absence of these factors are demotivators. Being paid a good wage and benefits and having a nice place to work doesn't result in people giving more effort, it just means the employer doesn't suck!

On the other hand, satisfier factors did contribute to an employee's motivation to give more effort and feel more passion for their job. Satisfiers are driven by company culture and management styles whereas hygiene factors are driven by company policy and programs.

Although this study was conducted in 1964, it is still very relevant today because human behavior has not changed since the study was conducted. What has changed are the management philosophies and approaches used to motivate employees. Just like the owner of the electrical contractor who thought that paying a good wage should be enough to motivate employees, many business owners still follow this archaic mindset and continue to be frustrated by the lack of passion in their company.

The high-tech industry was innovative when it started to change the physical workspace and environment. It went from people hiding in cubicles to open concepts, it offered meditation rooms and pool tables so everyone could have fun and relax. This strategy has migrated to other industries. I know of a construction company that has devoted twenty percent of its office space to recreation and relaxation spaces. At first glance these innovations look like they could be satisfier factors, but they are hygiene factors. These all make for a great work environment, but they don't necessarily result in opportunities for challenging work or career growth.

An employee doesn't need to have all the listed satisfier factors present to be motivated. Just as Mike Babcock expressed in his quote earlier in this chapter, the key is to understand what motivates each member of your team. Some members will be motivated by challenging work, some will seek recognition for their efforts while other will be motivated by being part of a common cause. Even the person who sweeps you shop floor and cleans toilets can be motivated if they understand how their efforts contribute to the greater good your company is trying to achieve. I cover much more about this in *Chapter 3, Empower Your Team with a Strategic Plan*.

Based on the needs of your team what changes can you make to incorporate more satisfier factors into your business? Here are a few ideas:

- Have regular meetings. They don't have to be long. Take ten or fifteen minutes to deal with any immediate challenges, review your core values and vision and most importantly, recognize someone on the team who went above and beyond their duties or at least demonstrated alignment with your company's culture.

- Have a foreman or lead hand run a meeting to develop their leadership skills.
- Find ways to challenge people with new tasks or use new skills. For example, if they only do rough ins have them do finishing work or change work stations so they can see the result of the work they do
- Proactively develop people so they take on new and exciting roles. Many people become energized when they see their peers getting ahead. It will motivate them to dig deeper so they can also get ahead at work and in life.
- Ensure that everyone understands the importance of their role in the big picture and how they are contributing to being part of making a positive change in your industry, community or even the world.

Take a hard look at your human resource programs and policies. Are they really satisfier factors or just hygiene factors? Are you truly motivating your team or does your company "just not suck"? You will be going in the right direction if you focus on developing your company's culture and improving your leadership style and management skills.

Chapter 3

Empower Your Company with a Powerful Strategic Plan

I can see clearly now

Just imagine if everyone in an organization arrived at work every day fully understanding the goals they wanted to achieve and how they were going to do it. Like a team of horses pulling a chariot everyone would be going in the same direction with all their energy dedicated to reaching the desired destination quicker than they ever imagined.

Every business or organization goes through occasional periods when they feel "stuck". There is a general feeling that the business is not moving forward, has little focus where everyone is working toward their own agenda. This can cause chaos in the organization resulting in low business performance and confused and demotivated staff. The answer to this disarray is to have a documented strategic plan.

Going through the strategic planning process can be very empowering for an organization. The process results in the focus and resolve for all members of the team to forge ahead and stay the course even during times of intense aversity.

Think of flying a plane at 30,000 feet. With a strategic plan you can see the horizon far ahead, you know your destination and how you are going to get there. As you look down you can see that there are towns and cities but are not necessarily able to identify the individual buildings and vehicles. At 10,000 feet, you can see more detail and can identify buildings and vehicles moving about. Whereas a Strategic Plan is a general long-term vision ranging from 3 to 5 years, a Business Plan is a shorter term (one year) action-oriented plan with more specific details on how to support the strategic plan. The strategic plan is the 30,000-foot view, the business plan is the 10,000-foot view and the execution of the plan is done at ground level.

There are six key steps when developing an effective and empowering strategic plan and they are covered in the following sections.

1.   Develop a Values/Vision/Mission Statements

This was covered in detail in Chapter 1 but for the sake of convenience here is a quick review:

> *Core Values* - Defines your values as it relates to integrity, work ethic, quality, treatment of others etc. This will set the tone and culture of your organization and will translate into how you and your team will treat all stakeholders.

> *Vision Statement* - Is an emotionally anchored statement that defines how your organization will have an impact on your industry, community or even society.

> *Mission Statement* – Mission Statement summarizes the actions your organization will take to achieve your vision while honoring your values.

2. *Conduct a SWOT Analysis*

SWOTT is an acronym for Strengths, Weaknesses, Opportunities, Threats and Trends. It is the process of assessing how your business is positioned for success right now and to determine what actions and strategies will be needed to flourish in the long term. A football team spends many hours developing a strategic plan that will help it to win the next game and to have a successful season. The coaching staff assesses the team's strengths and weaknesses. They will assess whether the defense is effective against the run or are they better positioned to defend against the pass. The offense will be assessed to determine if its strengths lie the running game or in the passing game. With the team's strengths and weaknesses identified the coaching staff can develop strategies to take advantage of opportunities by improving the team's weaknesses to reduce their vulnerabilities. On the other hand, they are can also look for opportunities to leverage their strengths to not only win the immediate game but to also have success for the current and even future seasons.

How many times have we heard a team described as not knowing their identity? A football team with an identity might be known as a passing team or having a swarming defense. When we can't recognize what a team excels at it is because they have no identity, nothing that brings the team together for a common cause. A team that lacks identity is a team without a strategic plan. They are rudderless, not understanding where they are going. Management, ownership and coaching are on different agendas causing confusion amongst the players and fans. Are you recognizing this in your business? Let's start working on your SWOTT.

Strengths

Identifying your strengths seems easy at first glance but many businesses take what they do well for granted and don't realize that they are doing some things better than their competition. Try comparing your company to the competition in areas such as delivery systems, technical knowledge, experience of staff, costs, efficiencies, logistics, marketing and sales power, unique manufacturing process or Intellectual Property (IP) to name just a few. You might surprise yourself with how your company is superior to your competition is certain areas.

Every company has at least one key strength it can leverage to take its business to the next level. What is yours? It often takes someone from outside your organization to recognize the strengths that you are overlooking so consider looking outside your organization for a different perspective.

<u>Weaknesses</u>

This requires some serious soul searching. Let's face it, who wants to admit their weaknesses. Think of the football team that recognizes it has a weak running game. If they ignore this weakness, the coaching staff might errantly develop a strategy that uses a lot of running plays resulting in less yards per play, less first downs and ultimately lower scores and more losses. On the other hand, a football team that recognizes this weakness will take action by looking for a better running back, improving blocking schemes or change the focus of the running back to protect the quarterback so the team will have more success passing the ball.

Just like the football team that decides to abandon the running game instead of propping it up, it is possible for a company to decide not to prop up its weakness but to instead focus its efforts on based on its strengths. I know of a company that identified personalized customer service as one of its strengths, but it required a lot of hands on attention from the customer service department. Their operating system was a little clunky requiring a lot of manual tracking that made it difficult to be profitable processing smaller sales as it took as much time to process a small sale as it took to process a large sale. A potential solution was to invest large amounts of money into a more automated system so small orders could be processed more efficiently. Management decided to continue to focus on personalized customer service but to spend most of their time focusing on larger orders and less transactions. Sales more than doubled in less than five years with profits quadrupling.

Be honest with yourself, what are your company's weaknesses? As you look at the list of possible strengths above are any of these your weaknesses? For example, are you slower at delivering your product than the competition or does your staff lack technical ability for knowledge? The longer the list the better. Eliminating just one weakness could be the difference between renewed success or continued frustration.

Opportunities

This is the fun part. It is time to start dreaming. Based on the strengths you identified earlier in this chapter start brain storming about all the possible opportunities and write them down. Don't worry about how crazy they may seem or how you will pursue them. You will create a short list later.

Amazon started out as an online book retailer. Management realized very early that its strengths did not lie in its book selection but it's ability to process orders very efficiently and to get the product to the customer very quickly and conveniently. It didn't matter what was in the shipping box, Amazon was very good at get that box to the customer. As a result, they are now an online powerhouse with sales over $178B in 2017 selling almost every type of product under the sun.

Based on your strengths are there new markets or products that you can focus on? Companies often find that there are huge opportunities within their existing market by making small adjustments. For example, if a company discovers that it can deliver a service much faster than its competitors it could change its sales and marketing message to focus on speed and pursue clients that value quick turnarounds and are willing to pay a premium for it.

Once you finish brainstorming opportunities based on your strengths go through the same process based on your weaknesses. If you were able to improve on your weaknesses what opportunities would be available that were not available before. There are times that a small incremental change can eliminate a weakness now creating a new opportunity.

Earlier in this chapter I described a company whose strength was providing personal customer service but had a clunky operating system. Rather than choosing to stay with higher valued sales they could have decided to prop up their weak operating system by investing in a more automated system that would allow them to process small orders more efficiently and profitably. This would have allowed them to pursue a whole new type of customer within their existing market and expand their business.

What more could you do if you addressed your company's weaknesses? If a weakness can be eliminated with little investment of time or money it might be worth it. If improving a weakness requires a more substantial investment, then it comes down to cost benefit analysis. You will have to determine if the net improvement will provide a desired return on investment.

Threats

These are factors that may or may not be beyond your control and includes both internal and external threats. An internal threat is something within your organization that could cause harm to your business. This includes a wide range of issues including labour unrest, health of a key person, ageing IT equipment or machinery to just name a few. The good news is that resolving internal threats is often within the control of management and if action is taken the threat can be neutralized.

External threats exist outside of your company but can have a detrimental effect on your business. Some possible external threats include government policies such as tariffs and industry regulations, economic conditions, currency exchange rates, disasters, attacks or competitive forces. In 2018/19 the American Government introduced tariffs on Canadian aluminum and steel. The Canadian Government introduced its own retaliatory tariffs. The result was that businesses on both sides of the border got caught in the cross fire adversely affecting their business and resorting to laying off employees. The tariffs were beyond the company's control, but it did affect their business.

List all the threats you can think of. How would you deal with each of these threats if they came to fruition? Don't let your business get blindsided. Having a plan for each threat ahead of time will allow you to react quicker, more decisively and hopefully even avoid the threats all together.

Fig 3.1

High Impact Low Investment	High Impact High Investment
Low Impact Low Investment	Low Impact High Investment

3. Develop Your Focus

So far you have your Vision, Mission and Values figured out and you have concluded your SWOT analysis. Chances are that you have a long list of opportunities to seize and threats to address. This can be overwhelming with all that information in front of you. The next step is to short list all the options for opportunities and threats to be addressed to three items each with a maximum of five depending on your company's size and ability to work on multiple items at a time.

Start by breaking the opportunities into four categories as shown in *Fig 3.1*: High Impact/Low Investment, High Impact/High Investment, Low Impact/Low Investment and Low Impact/High Investment. Which category would you start with? Hopefully your answer is High Impact/ Low Investment.

By having the team experience quick results with minimal resources allocated will build energy and commitment to the process not to mention you will benefit from the positive impact the changes have on business performance. The next category to work on is High Impact/ High Investment by conducting a cost/benefit analysis to determine viability. Unfortunately, too many companies devote too much time to either of the Low Impact categories. No company has unlimited resources, so it is very important to have the discipline to push those Low Impact items aside and focus on High Impact items only.

4. Create an Action Plan

The key to a successful Strategic Planning Process is turning all those great items on paper into tangible actions that result in positive change for your business. Follow these steps:

1. List each item you plan to pursue on a separate page in the form of a SMART goal.
2. List each step that must be taken to complete the item
3. Assign a deadline to each step
4. Assign the step to someone who is best suited to complete the step
5. Don't procrastinate, there never is a good time to start a project so start now!

Stating an action item as a SMART goal is very important to the process as it will give clear direction of what needs to be accomplished and increases accountability to be sure it gets done. SMART is an acronym for **S**pecific, **M**easurable, **A**ligned with core values, **R**ealistic and **T**ime Sensitive. For an intention to pass as a SMART goal it must pass all the criteria. A goal is not a SMART goal if any of the criteria is missing.

Specific – A goal must clearly state what the desired result with as much detail as possible. For example, if someone has a goal of buying a new car the goal should describe the make, model, year and even colour. The clearer the vision the better chance you have of achieving exactly what you want. A goal with a clear vision is already half way to being achieved.

Measurable – The goal needs to be quantifiable so you will know if you achieved the goal or whether you are on track to achieve it. A goal can be measured by growth percentage, profit level, customer or employee satisfaction ratings to name a few.

Aligned with Core Values - The "A" portion of a SMART goal is interesting as I have seen the "A" have different meanings to different people. I have seen it stated as "Achievable", "Actionable" and "Attainable" to just name a few. I prefer have goals aligned with core values because it keeps us honest with our selves. I heard a story of an executive who had a lifelong goal of being VP of Marketing for a large corporation. His goal was eventually achieved when he was offered the position as VP Marketing for a tobacco company. Although he was very qualified for the job it ate away at his conscience because both of his parents had died of lung cancer years earlier. The industry did not fit with his values. He eventually became depressed and had to take stress leave.

Realistic – If the person trying to achieve a goal feels that the chance of success is very slim or impossible, they will not be committed to the goal and will give up. There are two factors that can make a goal unrealistic. The first is aiming for a target so high that it seems humanly impossible to reach it. The other factor is timeline. Sometimes the target is within reach, but the amount of time given to reach it seems impossible. If you have a big audacious goal, try breaking into small bite size piece goals that seem more realistic.

Time Sensitive – An effective goal cannot be stated in perpetuity. There needs to be a defined date of when the goal is to be achieved otherwise, we will lack the sense of urgency and focus needed to see the goal come to fruition.

Let's practice writing a SMART goal. Many of us want to lose weight so let's write a SMART goal for losing weight. Which of the three goals below passes the SMART test?

I want to lose weight

I want to lose 20 pounds

I want to lose 20 pounds in 60 days from today

The correct answer is the 3rd statement but why not the first two? The first statement can be argued as specific but there is no measurement factor. The 2nd statement is measurable, but it has no timeline. The 3rd statement is specific enough and has a time line attached to it. How do we know if the goal is realistic? We must place into context of our current situation. If someone currently weighs 100lbs losing 20lbs might not be realistic whereas it might be realistic for a 200lbs person to not only lose 20lbs but to do it in 60 days.

Take time to scrutinize your goals statements very closely. It could be the difference between achievement or evaporating like a New Year resolution.

With your SMART goals clearly defined the next step is to break each goal down into action steps needed to achieve your goal. Using the weight loss goal of losing 20lbs in 60 days as an example my action steps might include researching three weight loss and exercise programs in the next five days, deciding which program to follow on day six and start on day seven. I would then establish a weekly mini goal of losing a certain amount of weight each week, so I could meet my objective in 60 days.

As you prepare to act on achieving your SMART goals be sure to list all action steps to be taken and that every step is assigned to the person best qualified to complete the step with deadlines clearly communicated. Plan to meet at appropriate intervals to measure progress and adjust the plan as necessary.

5. Communicate the Plan to Stakeholders

Now that your strategic plan has been finalized and documented it is now time to communicate the plan to your organization. Having great Mission, Vision and Values statements won't do you any good sitting in a binder. They need to be shared with everyone. Make your statements as visible as possible. Post them on your wall, on your website and in other promotional materials. Talk them up at every opportunity but remember, if your actions don't match the words the statements are worthless.

Share as much of your strategic plan as possible with the team so everyone understands what they can expect to happen and will want to contribute to your success. There will be specific details of the plan that need to be kept confidential. For example, if one of your goals is to reduce overhead by 20% you might make everyone on the team nervous because everyone knows that when there are cuts there are job losses. When people don't feel secure in their jobs, productivity and morale can take a nose dive. On the other hand, if one of your goals is to improve employee satisfaction, you will definitely want to share it.

6.   Monitor & Adjust

Don't let this happen to you. I have seen many companies that spend significant amounts of time and money developing a great strategic plan but when I ask to see it the document it is sitting under a bunch of papers with an inch dust on it. It's no surprise that these same companies don't think strategic plans work.

You must have an unwavering commitment to ensure that team meetings are held on a regular basis to monitor progress of action items and to ensure that goals are being achieved within the prescribed timelines. At the very least, there should be strategic plan update meetings every quarter. I would challenge you to meet every month if possible. They only need to be for an hour or two. The shorter the timelines between meetings the more likely that everyone will complete their tasks and achieve your goals. If goals and action items need to be adjusted to changing circumstance that is fine. Make any necessary adjustments and stay the course.

Chapter 4

Know Your Communication DNA

Who are you?

We already established in Chapter 2, *Be a Dynamic Leader,* that one of the most important skills of a great leader is communication. Besides working on communication skills with my own clients through our regular sessions or through my *Emerging Leaders Program,* I know many business coaches who also invest a significant amount of time developing their client's communication skills. This is so important that many leadership development programs start with assessing the leader's communication style before any other leadership qualities, so they can learn how to leverage this knowledge to become better communicators.

Have you ever had a conversation with someone and thought they either spoke too fast or too slow? Were they too blunt or just too friendly for your liking? It is because the other person has a different communication DNA than yours which can be annoying when we don't understand why they communicate that way. It doesn't have to be this way. By understanding the four basic communication styles we can adjust how we communicate in the moment to have a much more positive and productive interaction.

Fig 4.1

Compliance
Officer
Do: Speak slowly, give details
Back up claims with facts
Appeal to logic, Stay focused

Don't: Speak quickly,
Expect quick decisions
Keep changing subject
Spend a lot of time on small talk

Tasks

Director
Do: Be direct, stay on point
Present facts, speak quickly
Be confident and energetic

Don't: start with details
Back them into a corner
Show weakness, move slowly
Be unprepared

Introvert ← → **Extrovert**

Do: speak slowly, give details
Back up claims with facts
Be social, ask questions

Don't: speak quickly, forget promises
Keep changing subject
Make changes without warning
Be blunt, agressive

Do: Be positive, energetic
Engage in small talk
Be social, let them talk

Don't: Be negative, low energy
Get direct to the point
Talk too much, focus on details
Forget to show enthusiasm

Steady Eddie

Feeling

Influencer

Empowered Business Coaching ©2019

As shown in *Fig 4.1, Communication Styles,* there are four basic communication styles, each with its own characteristics of how the person with that style interacts with others. Although we are usually dominate in one or two styles, we all have our own unique combination of the four giving each of us our own communication DNA. Before we can talk about being a more effective communicator let's review the characteristics of the four styles.

Director – This person tends to be an extroverted task orient person and represents the stereotypical *Type A* personality. They are blunt and direct in how they communicate and tend to be very decisive. This type of leader can be successful in achieving results but can cause high employee turnover when not self-aware, due to their demanding style. They are impatient and prefer a fast cadence when communicating with others. They like to deal with the big picture and can become irritated when bogged down in too much detail. They will take back control of a project if they are not happy with progress.

The biggest strength of the Director is they are very clear about what they want to achieve. They don't take their eye off the ball and will keep the team focused as they progress toward their objective.

When communicating with a Director, it is important to understand that they deal with situations and not people so don't take their blunt style personally. When communicating with them be direct and focus on results. Only give them detail if they ask for it. Directors look for confidence and conviction in people so be sure to display this if you want your message accepted. They make decisions quickly by trusting their gut and determining how their decision will allow them to achieve their goal.

Influencer – Usually known as a "people person" and being very social this leader usually displays high energy and wants a positive atmosphere. They achieve results by connecting with people at a emotional level and personal level, wanting everyone to be happy. They show their emotions openly and are often described as "wearing their emotions on their sleeve". The downside of the Influencer is they can struggle holding others accountable or having tough conversations because of potential negativity and fear of no longer being popular. Like the Director, Influencers are also not detail oriented and see details as a "downer" and energy sucker.

When communicating with Influencers try to be positive, smile and stick with the big picture. Take time to build rapport at a human level by engaging in small talk and asking questions about them. Influencers like to express themselves so let them talk as much as possible although you might have to cut off the conversation, so you can move on to the job at hand. They make decisions quickly by relying on their intuition and how they feel about the person they are interacting with.

Steady Eddy – This leader tends to be more thoughtful and introspective than the other styles. They do not usually display high energy, but they do inspire others by showing empathy. Achieving consensus and valuing input from their team is one of their biggest strengths. They are good listeners and can control a conversation by asking relevant questions. Being averse to making mistakes and to change, they tend to make decisions slowly, relying on facts and past results rather than relying on their gut and intuition.

People who like to work in a stable and harmonious environment will appreciate the Steady Eddy. Those who prefer a faster paced and ever-changing environment may get frustrated by the slower pace and very stable environment. They don't like conflict or aggressive behavior in others so they will try to avoid heated debates that could have otherwise resulted in creative solutions.

<u>Compliance Officer</u> – Being very analytical, this leader can be quite introverted and is most effective when there are strong systems in place. Attention to detail is so important to them that they struggle with the big picture and get very frustrated when systems are not followed. Often suffering from "paralysis through analysis" the compliance officer is most comfortable making decisions based on detailed facts and figures rather than their gut or intuition. They strive for perfection. They fear losing control and will micro manage their team if not self-aware.

People who prefer an environment with strong systems, predictability and detailed direction will thrive under this leader. Those who prefer flexibility and autonomy will find themselves frustrated with the restrictive nature of a Compliance Officer lead team.

Which Style is Best?

If you are thinking that no communication style is the best leader you are correct. A leader can be successful regardless of their style. Just like all other areas of leadership development the key is self- awareness. By understanding the strengths and weaknesses of our communication DNA and by learning how to recognize the communication style of others we have the power to adjust our communication style to communicate more effectively.

Fig 4.2

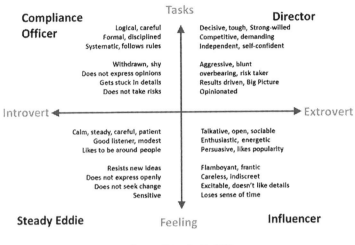

As shown in *Fig 4.2*, there are specific adjustments that a leader can make in the moment when communicating with those with different styles. For example, the Director can try to communicate with a Steady Eddy in a way that is most comfortable to the Steady Eddy. They should speak more slowly and include supporting information for their statements in their conversation. The Compliance Officer can try to increase their energy and positivity when communicating with an Influencer. No one expects someone to be something they are not but by adjusting as much as we can we can close the communication gap enough to get the best possible outcome from our interaction.

The best leaders recognize their shortcomings and surround themselves with people who possess the attributes they don't have. The Director will be sure to have people who are sensitive to the human side when making decisions and with those who pay more attention to detail. The Influencer will benefit from having detailed oriented people and those that will drive the team to success. The Steady Eddy will want those who bring more energy and directiveness to the team.

The Compliance Officer will also want those who bring more energy and a human component to the team.

Do you recognize yourself or your staff members in any of these styles? If you can adjust how you communicate based on the other person's style so they are comfortable and open to new ideas, you will be surprised by how much more buy-in you get when resolving issues or motivating them to give their best effort as they pursue company goals. They will be more likely to rally around your Mission and Vision and while adhering to your Core Values.

Section II

The Magic Profit Formula

Chapter 5

How the Formula Works

One step at a time

Warning, there is a profitability epidemic out there. After meeting with over a hundred business owners I am shocked by how many well established, reputable businesses are not making a profit. I am sure that one of the reasons you started or bought your business was to make a profit. It's your reward for the financial risk you took not to mention the challenges that come with business ownership.

Every business owner wants to improve their profits, but it's easier said than done, or is it? I use a straight forward formula when working with my clients that I call *The Magic Profit Formula* to turn a business around.

The "formula" can be applied to virtually any business, in any industry to improve profitability and overall business performance. It is often not necessary to make sweeping changes to a business to see big results. A company can realize exceptional improvements to business performance by making only small incremental changes and adjustments to each part of the business process. Achieving just a 10% incremental improvement at each step will compound into <u>a **71%** increase in profits.</u>

Fig 5.1

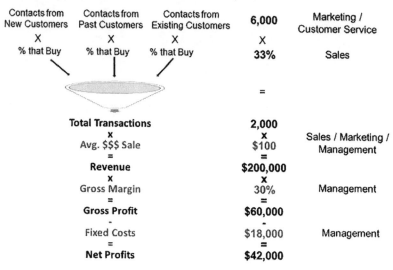

The Magic Profit Formula

Contacts from New Customers	Contacts from Past Customers	Contacts from Existing Customers	6,000	Marketing / Customer Service
X	X	X	X	
% that Buy	% that Buy	% that Buy	33%	Sales

Total Transactions	2,000	
x	x	Sales / Marketing / Management
Avg. $$$ Sale	$100	
=	=	
Revenue	$200,000	
x	x	
Gross Margin	30%	Management
=	=	
Gross Profit	$60,000	
-	-	
Fixed Costs	$18,000	Management
=	=	
Net Profits	$42,000	

As shown in *Fig 5.1*, the standard business process is broken down nine steps: Customer Attraction (Leads), Sales Conversion, Number of Customers, Average Sale, Revenue, Gross Margin, Gross Profit, Fixed Costs and Net Profit. The numbers in the example are not based on a specific business and are for demonstration purposes only. Let's take a detailed look at each step as we run through the numbers.

Customer Attraction is the marketing process. The only purpose of marketing is to attract *qualified* potential customers (leads) to your business. I will get into more detail on how this is done in Chapter 6 when I cover Marketing. The formula starts by accounting for how many leads that either call you, sends an online enquiry or walks into your location. The leads are broken down into three categories: *New Customers, Existing Customers* and *Past Customers,* with each category having its own specific strategy for attraction. In our example there are a total of 6000 leads from all three categories.

Sales Conversion is the process of converting a lead into a sale. It is calculated by dividing the *Number of Transactions* by *Total Leads* produced and stated as a percentage.

$$\underline{Number\ of\ Transactions}\ X\ 100 = Sales\ Conversion\ Rate$$
$$Total\ Leads$$

To illustrate how the above conversion formula works, let's assume below that 6000 leads came into your business last month resulting in 2000 transactions. Your sales conversion rate would be 33%.

$$\underline{2000\ (Transactions)}\ X\ 100 = 33\%$$
$$6000\ (Leads)$$

Once a lead has reached out to you there must be a process for converting that lead into a paying customer. All efforts should focus on helping the potential customer with their decision-making process, so they can make an informed decision about whether to buy your product or service. Each lead category will have its own conversion rate based on the customer's familiarity with your business and the complexity of the conversion of that customer. For example, marketing to past customers will usually have a higher conversion rate than new customers. I know of an electrical services company that receives calls for service on daily basis from brand new customers and customers that have dealt with them before. After tracking calls for a few months, we determined that the conversion rate for past customers was 85% while only 55% of new customer enquiries converted into sales. There was an obvious issue with the sales conversion process so we made the necessary adjustments and were able to improve the conversion rate to 70%, so as you can see it is important to track each type of lead separately. I will talk more about this in Chapter 7, *Be a Sales Warrior*.

The *Number of Transactions* is derived from your sales or invoice registry. To be sure that you know your conversion rates by lead type you will need a system to track the origin on the sale

The *Average Sale* is calculated simply by dividing your Total Revenue by the Total number of invoices generated. For example, if sales for a period was $200,000 with 2000 invoices generated, the average sale would be $200,000/2000 = $100.

$$\frac{Total\ Revenue}{Number\ of\ Invoices} = Average\ Sale$$

Total Revenue is taken directly from your sales registry.

Gross Margin is *Gross Profit* stated as a percentage of sales. Gross Profit is calculated by subtracting the Cost of Goods Sold from Sales. This is covered in more detail in Chapter 12, *Understanding Financial Management* but for your convenience, I have provided a quick review below.

$$Revenue - Cost\ of\ Goods\ Sold = Gross\ Profit$$

$$\frac{Gross\ Profit}{Revenue} \times 100 = Gross\ Margin$$

For example, if you sold a product or service for $100 and the cost to produce the product or fulfill the service was $67 your Gross Profit would be $33 (Selling Price – Cost of Goods Sold). The Gross Margin is 33% (Gross Profit/Selling Price).

$$\$100\ (Revenue)-\$67\ (Cost\ of\ Goods\ Sold) = \$33\ (Gross\ Profit)$$

$$\frac{\$33\ (Gross\ Profit)}{\$100\ (Revenue)} \times 100 = 33\%\ (Gross\ Margin)$$

Fixed Costs are also covered in more detail in Chapter 12, but just to quickly review, Fixed Costs are those costs that you incur whether you sell product or serve a customer or not and they usually do not fluctuate very much from period to period unless there was a significant change to the business. Some of the most common Fixed Costs include rent, office & management salaries, phone, interest, insurance etc.

Net Profit is that number we all look forward to seeing. This is your return for taking the risk of investing in your business, not to mention for all of your hard work. It is calculated by subtracting all those Cost of Goods Sold and Fixed Expenses from Revenue.

Which area do you think I start with when working with a new client? You might be surprised to hear that I usually start with Gross Profits. The reason is simple. Of all the businesses I have analyzed I found that a large percentage already had enough revenue to be profitable. The "low hanging fruit" to improve profits quickly were very often sitting in gross profits.

Making the Formula Work

Although I often start with Gross Profits, for the sake of simplicity we will start at the beginning of the formula. In example shown in *Fig 5.1*, the marketing program currently produces 6000 leads. With a combined conversion rate of 33% as shown in the left column, the total number of transactions are 2000. By dividing total revenue of $200,000 by the number of transactions (2000) we know that the average sale size is $100.

In this example, the accounting software reports that Gross Margins are 30%. When we multiply $200,000 in sales by the 30% margin, we end up with $60,000 in Gross Profit. The accounting software also confirms that Fixed Costs (Overhead) is currently $18,000 leaving a Net Profit of $42,000.

Fig 5.2

The Formula in Action

	Before	After
Number of Leads	**6,000**	**6,600**
x	x	x
Conversion Rate	33%	36.3%
=	=	=
No. of Customers	**2,000**	**2,396**
x	x	x
Avg. $$$ Sale	100	110
=	=	=
Revenue	**200,000**	**263,560**
x	x	x
Margin	30%	33%
=	=	=
Gross Profit	**60,000**	**87,975**
-	-	-
Fixed Costs	18,000	16,200
=	=	=
Net Profits	**42,000**	**71,775**

So here is where the "magic" begins. In *Fig 5.2*, we can see the effect each step has on the business process if we were to make a 10% incremental improvement to each step. Notice how if we increase the number of leads by 10% from 6000 to 6600 and if we increase the conversion rate by 10% from 33% to 36.3% that the total number of transactions increases from 2000 to 2396. Now let's get crazy and increase the average sales size by 10% from $100 to $110. Sales now increase by 32% to $263,560. How can this be? How do 10% increases result in a 32% increase in sales? It's the power of compounding. As we increase each step by 10% it compounds with the subsequent steps to create a snowball effect. It works the same as compounding interest in your bank account or investment.

Let's say that you invest $1000 and get a return of 5% per year compounded each year. How much would you have after letting the invest sit for five years? Most would say $1250 but the answer is $1276.29. When we say that an investment will return 5%, compounded annually it means that the investment will return 5% based on the balance at the start of the year. As you can see in in the chart below, when the return rate is based on previous returns it accelerates the growth. The same happens when ten percent increases are added to previous ten percent increases. It accelerates the growth. It's like magic!

Year Ending	Interest Earned	New Balance
Initial Deposit	N/A	$1000
1	$50.00	$1050
2	$52.50	$1102.50
3	$55.13	$1157.63
4	$57.88	$1215.51
5	$60.78	$1276.29

The magic doesn't stop here. Look at what happens when we increase Gross Margins by 10% from 30% to 33%. Gross Profits now increase from $60,000 to $87,975, a 46% increase!! Now let's take the opposite approach with Fixed Costs. If we reduce Fixed Costs by 10% from $18,000 to $16,200 and combine this with the other 10% improvements already made, Net Profits increase from $42,000 to $71,775 or a 71% improvement.

The key is to work on only one step at a time. Put your blinders on and focus solely on improving the performance of that one step by 10% which at the end of the day is a small improvement to make. Now Its's time to brain storm again just like we did during the SWOT analysis back in Chapter 3. Write down every idea you can think of to improve the outcomes of the step you are working on. If possible, get your team involved and list all the ideas on a board or flip chart. Remember, no idea is too crazy. You will short list later.

Once all possible ideas are listed it's time to start whittling the list down to the strategies you plan to move forward with. Use the matrix shown in Fig *3.1* in Chapter 3 to help you decide which strategies to use. Are there any strategies that require minimal investments of time and resources that would provide a significant and measurable outcome? If so, then start with those. Try to keep your short list down to 3 – 5 strategies. It will help to keep everyone focused and increase the probability of an effective and successful execution, so you can meet or exceed your goal of a 10% improvement for that step.

Chapter 6

Generate More Leads with Marketing

Finding needles in the haystack

As mentioned in the previous chapter, marketing is defined as the process of generating enough interest from <u>qualified</u> prospects so they will inquire about your product. The inquiries can be in the form of phone calls, emails, filling in inquire forms or the prospect walking into your location. Once the qualified prospect has reached out, marketing has done its job. Converting the lead into a sale is part of the sales process which we will cover in the next chapter.

First, let's acknowledge that marketing is a black hole for most small business owners. Finding new customers is like looking for a needle in a haystack. Huge amounts of money are thrown at various strategies often with very disappointing results and little, if any return, on investment. It's no wonder that most business owners see marketing as a waste of money and give up, vowing to never spend money on marketing again. The reason that most marketing strategies fail is because the fundamental process of developing a marketing plan was not followed.

There are three distinctive steps to developing a marketing program that includes (1) Identify your Ideal Customer (2) Craft a Message that Speaks Directly to Your ideal Customer (3) Decide how You will Get Your Message to Your Ideal Customer.

Stop Marketing Zebras

When I speak with business owners who are frustrated with marketing I always ask the question "who is your ideal client?" The answer usually starts with "anyone" which is the first sign of trouble.

I learned a marketing rule many years ago which is still very relevant today. Here it is, *"anyone who tries to make everyone their customer ends up with no one as a customer."*

Here is an example. Let's assume that you sell horses. In the horse market there are people who want white horses and those who want black horses. As a marketer you are asking yourself "how can I sell a product to all of these people"? You have a brilliant idea. You will market zebras. They are perfect. They are black and white, both types of customers will be happy, or will they?

You jump right in, invest tons of money in marketing and start to market your zebras. Oh no! No one is buying. What's going on? Everyone should be happy! After some research you find out that the people who want white horses don't want horses with black on them and the people who want black horses don't want any white on them. They prefer solid colours. By trying to make everyone happy you made no one happy. You didn't completely satisfy the wants and needs of either type of customer, so they didn't buy.

When we take the time to research and identify the specific needs and wants of our ideal clients, we can then develop a product mix and market messaging that is aimed directly at the people we want to serve. The more specific the message the more likely it will resonate with our market and will end up with a positive response. Our potential clients are being exposed to hundreds of marketing stimuli every day, so our message must hit them between the eyeballs with a concise message that is relevant to them.

Invest some time to fully understand exactly what your target market wants from you and adjust your product mix and messaging aimed only at them. If done effectively you will see your business grow faster than ever.

"Dare to Declare" Your Ideal Client

Being able to identify your ideal client and understanding their needs and wants is foundational to effective marketing. Ideal clients have a deeper desire for your product than the rest. They benefit more from your product than others and will usually pay a higher price because they see and understand the value you offer. You are probably wondering how to identify these people from the rest of the pack. The first step is to create an Avatar of your ideal client, so you have a tangible form to represent them.

To create an avatar of your ideal client, create a chart similar to the one shown in *Figure 6.1*. Write in "Client" in the top left header then label each of the remaining headers with criteria that best describes your Avatar e.g. Age, Gender, Geographic Location, Income, Occupation, Industry etc. Next, make a list of your top 20 customers and complete the chart with one customer per line. Once all the information is entered review each column to determine if about 80% of your top customers have the same or similar information. If they do, then this becomes part of your Avatar. If 80% of the customers don't share the same dynamic in that column then that criteria are not relevant in developing your Avatar.

Let's look at the example in *Fig 6.1*. In this example we have a company that services small and medium size businesses. They created a chart and decided to use the following criteria to build the profile of their top seven client to develop their Avatar: *Number of Employees, Sales, Geographic location, Number of Sales People on their Team and whether they have their own IT department or not.*

As you scan down each column do you see any patterns? Are there any columns where 80% (about 5 out of 7) clients listed have similar or the same data in that column? Let's take a look at one column at a time. In the *Number of Employees* column, 5 of the 7 clients have between 10 and 20 employees with two having 35 or more. We can assume that the best clients have between 10 and 20 employees since 5 of 7 were in a similar range. The 2nd column to qualify is the *Sales* column. In this case 5 of 7 clients have sales between $1M and $2M while two clients have sales of $10M+. We can conclude that the ideal client has sales between $1M and $2M. In the *Area* column the pattern is not as apparent. We have four clients in New York, two in Florida and one in California. There isn't the magic 5 of 7 of one area however we could assume that 6 of 7 are on the east coast which could be part of the Avatar. We might want to look at more clients to confirm this.

Fig 6.1

Company	# Emp	Sales	Area	Industry	# Sales People	IT Dep			
A	10	$1M	New York	Distribution	1	No			
B	35	$10M	Florida	MFG	3	Yes			
C	14	$1.5M	California	Distribution	2	Yes			
D	45	$14M	Florida	MFG	4	Yes			
E	13	$1.1M	New York	Retail	2	No			
F	15	$1.5M	New York	MFG	2	Yes			
g	19	$1.8M	California	Service	2	Yes			

In the *Industry* column there also doesn't seem to be a clear pattern with only two clients in distribution, three in manufacturing and the last two splits between retail and services. There might be a possibility that the Avatar would be in manufacturing or distribution since the two sectors often work together. Again, we need to confirm this with looking at more of our top existing clients.

In the *Number of Sales People* column there also doesn't seem to be a clear pattern although it appears that the Avatar will have between one and four sales people.

In the *IT Department* column, we can see that 5 of 7 clients do have an IT department with only 2 not having one, so having an IT department would most likely be part of the Avatar.

What can we conclude with this exercise? Our Avatar is in the manufacturing or distribution business, has ten to twenty employees, sales of $1M to $2M, is located on the east coast, has one to four sales people and does have an IT department.

Try the same process if you serve the Business to Consumer (B to C) market. The only difference will be the criteria you use to determine your Avatar. For example, instead of sales you might use income. Instead of industry you might use occupation etc. With this knowledge in place you can start making some decisions on how and where to market so your message will reach *qualified* prospects that share the same profile as your best and most profitable clients

Once you have a clear picture of who your ideal client is, the next step is to understand their psychographics. This is harder to identify because you can't identify it based on the same information, we used to identify demographics. To understand someone's psychographics, we need to get inside their head. We need to understand what is going on in their lives. What do they worry about the most? What keeps them up at night? With this information in hand you can start answering questions like how can your product make their life easier? What would motivate them to buy your product? Etc. You can get this information through direct discussions with your existing or past clients or through surveys. Understanding your ideal client's psychographics is just as important as knowing their demographics because it is key to developing a laser focused message that will get their attention no matter how many ads or stimuli they are expose to every day.

Craft a Laser Focused Message

We are exposed to literally hundreds of ads and commercials as we read magazines, watch TV or just driving down the street and suddenly one grabs our attention. We stop and read the ad or watch the commercial then decide whether to act on it or not. Why did that one ad stop us in our tracks while barely noticing all the others we were exposed to? The answer is simple. The key message in the ad we responded to was directly relevant to what was going on in our life at that time.

An ad that promises a more youthful look will resonate with someone who is concerned about ageing or an ad that portrays someone relaxing on a beach will grab the attention of someone who is thinking about taking a vacation. If we are not concerned about looking more youthful or taking a vacation at the time we saw the ad it is very unlikely we will notice it or at the very least we will pay little attention to it.

There is a definite art to crafting a laser focused message, but it also involves some science. There is mathematical proof that you can literally triple the probability of success of your marketing program by ensuring it includes the following key components.

1. Your message must communicate an OVERT Benefit
2. There must be a REASON TO BELIEVE
3. There must be a REAL DRAMATIC DIFFERENCE

In his book *Jump start Your Business Brain*, Doug Hall explains how he discovered these crucial components by itemizing the marketing components of 4000 successful and not successful opportunities and then created a computer program that could forecast the probability of success. Doug Hall found that opportunities that had all 3 of the key components had triple the success rate compared to those that did not have them. Let's take a more detailed look at each component.

Overt Benefit – You might have heard of features and benefits. A feature is a statement that identifies what the product has within it.

A benefit states what the feature does. For example, when looking at a brochure for a new car it might state that it has an Automatic Braking System. This is a feature since it simply identifies what it is. The Benefit is that it automatically applies the brakes if the system senses that the driver will not apply the brakes in time.

Most marketing fails because it only communicates features with only a few communicating actual benefits. Features and benefits are statements of fact and appeal to logic only. An OVERT benefit is like a benefit on steroids and triggers an emotional response vs a logical response. It communicates the most positive and maximum effect the product will have on the person's life if they buy the product. An example of a benefit for a cleaning product might be "saves you time and money" whereas an OVERT benefit might say "start cleaning at 9 and be on the golf course by 11". In the example of the Automatic Braking System the Overt Benefit might be "keep your family safe".

Listing the features and benefits of your product(s) is relatively easy since they are just statements of fact. Determining the Overt Benefit is not so easy since it is based on an emotional statement rather than a factual statement. The first step is to know the psychographics of the targeted customer to understand their emotional state and only then can you attempt to develop an Overt Benefit statement that will trigger an emotional response.

Reason To Believe – How many times have you responded to an advertisement in the newspaper, TV or online because the advertiser promised fantastic or life changing results. Perhaps a cleaning products manufacturer claimed that its product would clean better than anything else on the market or that exercise program promised you would lose 20 lbs. in 30 days sculpting you into a head turning specimen. How did that go by the way? We have all been disappointed with products that over promised and under delivered leaving us very suspicious of future claims and accepting them with a grain of salt.

One of my earliest experiences as a disappointed consumer was when I was eight years old. I saw an ad in a comic book that said, "learn how to throw your voice and fool your friends, become a ventriloquist". I thought how fun this would be, I could make boxes and other objects look like they could talk. My friends and family would be baffled. I saved up my allowance money and sent in my five dollars plus shipping and handling. After a few weeks of anticipation, it finally arrived. I opened the little package and all it contained was an instruction sheet with a diagram and a little metal spacer to put between my lips, so they would be partially opened, forcing me to talk without moving my mouth. That's right, I paid five dollars for a little piece of metal. I was so disappointed that I vowed to never buy anything from a comic book again and no matter how good a product looked in the ad, I always thought about that disappointment and didn't respond to another ad again.

I am sure you could spend hours or even days talking about products you bought where the advertiser's claim caused you to have high expectations only to be left very disappointed with the reality. Perhaps it was buying one of those "slicer dicer" products you saw on TV that just didn't work as well as shown in the demonstration or perhaps you responded to a newspaper ad for a plumbing service that promised a one-hour response but didn't show up for four hours. Both might have made claims that sounded good but ended up falling well short of your expectations. We have learned to not believe most of what we see or hear from advertisers which makes it very challenging for the advertiser to convince someone to respond to the ad no matter great their products.

How do we convince a potential customer to believe our Overt Benefit statement, so they will respond to our advertisement? The secret is to back up your OVERT benefit with a *real reason to believe*. This is a statement that appeals to logic by stating indisputable factual information to back up your claim. In the case of the slider dicer on TV It might try to convince you that it is so good that "guarantees satisfaction or money refunded within 30 days". The plumber promising a one-hour response might say "we will arrive in 60 minutes or the first hour is on us". In both cases you might be inclined to think, "if they are backing up their claim that much, it just might be true", and you would be more likely to respond to the ad.

A real reason to believe doesn't necessarily have to be in the form of guarantees. Depending on the nature of your product and value to the customer, claims can also include, "based on scientific research", "over 10,000 happy customers" or "made of high-grade aircraft aluminum". In each case respectively a person might conclude that a product designed based on science is more likely to work, a company with many happy customers must do a great job or a product made of aircraft aluminum must be of the highest quality since it is the same material that airplanes are made from.

What does your company produce or do that you are so proud of and would offer such high value to a customer that you could back up your Overt Benefit to the point that you could remove any doubt or apprehension that would cause them to not act on your advertisement? This could be the missing piece of your marketing puzzle.

Real Dramatic Difference – All of your competition is trying to convince your current or potential customers to buy from them instead of you every single day as they bombard the market place with messages and enticing offers. We already know that your message needs to communicate an Overt Benefit and be backed up with a Real Reason to Believe. The secret to cutting through all the rhetoric is to ensure that your offer is dramatically different from your competition. Ask yourself "how can I solve a problem or address a frustration differently from the competition?

Dramatic differences can be divided into four categories: *speed, convenience, quality* and *price.* Is your competition failing to address one or more of these characteristics? Residential telecommunication companies used to tell their customers that they would arrive on a certain day but with no commitment on arrival time to install a new product or to fix a problem. This meant the customer would have to take a day off work and sit around all day, not knowing when the technician would arrive leaving the customer extremely frustrated and inconvenienced. Some telecommunication companies recognized this frustration and started offering appointments with two-hour arrival windows. Now the customer could plan their day better knowing they would not have to hang around all day. This went a long way to addressing a widely known frustration with the industry. By making it easier to do business with the telco, customers were much more likely to choose them over the competition that did not offer this convenience.

Amazon has taken online ordering to a whole new level. Many people love the convenience of ordering online but were frustrated having to wait days or weeks to receive their exciting new product. Recognizing this frustration Amazon configured their systems so they were able to offer same day or next day delivery for many of their products. This has been unbelievably successful and has created a spin off industry of same day delivery services.

Do you already offer a product or have configured your product, so it is very different than your competition? If not, what changes can you make to differentiate yourself? Would your customers see value in getting your product faster, easier or having other features than would solve a frustration that no one else is solving. If so, be sure to make it the focal point of your marketing message.

Get Your Message Out

Even the most expertly crafted marketing message is worthless unless your ideal clients see or hear it. Small businesses spend thousands of dollars to get their well-crafted messages out to market with little to no results to show for their investment. Choosing how to get your message to ideal clients can be hit and miss but you can improve your chance of success by following these steps:

1. Review the avatar of your ideal client that you created earlier in this chapter.
2. Based on their profile and using the criteria below, determine which medias give you the best chance of reaching your ideal clients for the least cost.
    a. Where do they live or work?
    b. Where do they congregate (associations, chamber, clubs, activities)?
    c. What newspaper, magazines or blogs do they read?
    d. Are they on social media or online groups?
    e. Where else do they shop for related products?

If your clients work or live in a concentrated area try to choose advertising products that specialize in that area. You are not likely to get a favorable return on your advertising dollar if you pay for exposure to a whole country when all your business is in one city. If your clients have a shared interest in a certain topic such as sports or the arts, there is media such as magazines, social media pages, TV shows and blogs that specialize in reaching these markets.

We can't forget your online strategy. It is well documented that many consumers have turned away from traditional print media or TV to online media to acquire information. Besides the shift in consumer behavior, one of the biggest reasons that advertisers are diverting more marketing resources to online media is that it gives even the smallest business the opportunity to target their ads to a specific customer so there is little to no money spent on wasted exposure. Social media platforms such as Facebook and LinkedIn allow the advertiser to target their ads and advertising budget to people or business with specific characteristics. You can choose to have your ads displayed based on gender, age, area, interests, industry, company size, occupation etc.

Online media and its associated technologies are changing daily. There is a lot to know. I'm sure that your strengths lie in other areas of your business besides marketing. It would pay to have a qualified marketing person or service help you if you are not confident with it.

Be very critical of where you spend your marketing dollars. Have the discipline to only invest in media that specializes in communicating with your ideal customer.

Be Aware of Space Sellers

Have you ever received a cold call or been approached by a sales person who sells advertising products? Isn't it odd that no matter what business you are in, their media is perfect for your business?

There is no doubt that advertising can be very effective if you choose the right media for your business and the messaging is tailored to resonate with your target audience. There are some real advertising pros out there that truly understand marketing and how their advertising product can fit with your business. On the other hand, there are many people who know very little about marketing and are just trying to sell space whether it's print, digital or the airwaves.

So how do you tell the difference between the "space sellers" and the true marketers? Here are a few ideas:

1. First you need to understand who your ideal client is and what they read, watch or listen to.
2. Ask the advertising rep who the target audience of their media is. If they say "everyone" or don't give you a clear and concise answer stop the conversation and run away as far and fast as you can because you are dealing with a "space seller". The fact is that every media knows who the audience of their product is. There are various tracking systems used by the media industry that provides them with feedback on their target audience and the number of people that it reaches. Advertising reps have either not been properly trained or don't want to say the wrong thing, so they lose the sale. In either case this is a sign that you are dealing with a "space seller"

3. I like to have fun with advertising sales people. When they say their product "is the perfect media for my business" I usually respond by saying," great, so who is my ideal customer". In my more than thirty years in business I have never had one advertising rep able to tell me who my ideal customer is, so how do they know their product is right for my business? They don't. Their selling space, not marketing.

A true marketing pro will take the time to ask you about your business, what market you are trying to serve and who your ideal customer is. If they truly have the right product for your business, they will be able to back it up with numbers and research. If they can't back up their claims, then save your money.

I have also offered different media sales people "pay for performance" plans where I would pay them a lucrative commission for every sale their product generates. I have even shown them how they will make much more money with the incentive plan than their standard fixed fee if their media is truly as effective as they claim. This is sometimes done in the Direct Response marketing fields, but most media will not do it. I wonder why?

4. If you ask, "how can I measure the results" and the rep says, "its hard to measure results, it's about getting your name out there", you have a potential "space seller". Unless you have a very large company with deep pockets it is unlikely that advertising just to "get your name out there "is feasible. This is a sign that the rep is trying to avoid accountability for the performance of their product. If you can't measure it, don't do it.

Companies lose enormous amounts of money due to ineffective marketing. We are never going to be 100% accurate with our marketing decisions but if you ask some of these questions, stay disciplined and are firm in your expectations you will invest your marketing dollars much more effectively.

Chapter 7

Be a Sales Warrior

My bucket runneth over

We have already talked about how marketing is the nemesis of most small business owners, a necessary evil that rarely seems to translate into measurable sales. The fact is that the marketing program may not be problem when it comes to generating sales.

The sole purpose of marketing is to generate qualified leads. It has done its job once a qualified prospective customer calls, emails or walks into your business and expresses interest in your product or service.

How many times have you received a call from a potential customer and fumbled with the call? Perhaps you immediately started talking about your product assuming you already knew their needs or gave your price right away to only have the prospect hang up or walk out with a polite "thank you, I will get back to you." It might have cost you hundreds of dollars to generate that inquiry and in a moment, they are gone with nothing to show for your marketing investment. I am sure that you have also been that customer that responded to a marketing message to only walk away during the sales process because you didn't feel the vendor really cared about your needs.

My experience has shown that most companies spend very little resources measuring or developing a system to maximize the conversion rate of Leads to Sales. Your sales system is as important to your company's success as an effective marketing program. It is imperative that when a prospect responds to a marketing message they are taken through a consistent and orchestrated buying process that will produce predictable results.

During my years as a sales manager and even as I provide sales training today as part of my business coaching practice, I have discovered the one common denominator that held back most sales people from success. They didn't have a sales process and "winged" it hoping the product would somehow sell itself. Most sales people would gather up their brochures, head off to the prospects office or home and present all the great features of their product. They would conduct a great presentation but would leave frustrated without an order.

The key to sales success is to understand that there is a decision-making process the buyer must go through before they agree to buy. The sales person who understands the sales process and who can successfully guide the prospect through the process will achieve success.

The Trust Model of Selling

Fig 7.1

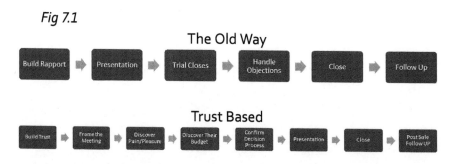

There is a hilarious movie from the late eighties called *Tin Men* Staring Richard Dreyfuss and Danny DeVito that follows the antics of two aluminum siding salesmen as they try to convince people they needed new aluminum siding on their home. The two characters spend all kinds of time trying to trick or manipulate people into buying their product. This is an extreme look how sales people conducted themselves at the time, but the reality is the portrayal of sales people in the movie wasn't too far from the truth at the time. Until about the mid-nineties the sales model was based on finding people who could be interested in your product and then convincing them to buy by showering them with all its great features then using all kinds of methods to handle objections and all kinds of tips and tricks to close the sale.

Sales methods started to change significantly in the early nineties as consumers became more aware of the tricks of the sales trade and would share their experiences through numerous online chatrooms and other online platforms. *As shown in Figure 7.1*, the old system would involve taking just enough time to establish the rapport needed so the meeting would go well enough to end in a closed sale. With this superficial relationship set the sales person would go into the presentation telling the prospect about all the great things the product could do. We used to call this the "dog & pony show". A little sales trick people often used was to keep asking the prospect questions that he would answer "yes" to. The questions were often basic like, "do you want to save money"? We all want to save money, so the answer was always "yes". With the prospect now conditioned to say "yes", the sales person would a do a trial close. This is when the sales person would ask questions to see if the prospect was ready to buy. Typical questions asked were "which colour do you prefer" or "when would you like it delivered"? The prospect either said what they preferred which indicated they were ready to buy, or they would respond with objections as to why they couldn't buy. This is where the games began. The sales person would ask what their concerns were and then provide the answer to neutralize the objection. The sales person would eventually answer all the questions or overcome the prospects concerns and apprehensions to the point that there was no longer an excuse to not buy. The sale person would close the sale. It is clear to see the games that were being played between the sales person and prospect. There were and still are sales training programs that teach fifty ways to close a sale. Those days are gone. Whereas the old-style model would spend 10% of the process on building just enough rapport to close the sale, the current sales model is based on spending 40% of the process on building genuine trust.

Follow along with *Fig 7.1* as I explain each step of the current trust model in more detail.

1. **Build a High Trust Relationship.** As we already know, building trust is foundational to a successful sales interaction, yet many sales people don't do it effectively. Many sales people will stumble through small talk as they awkwardly transition to the business at hand. Talking about the weather only goes so far. The best way to build rapport is to be prepared. It doesn't matter whether your customers call you, meets you at your location or if you see the client in their location the key is to have a repertoire of appropriate greetings you can use to make them immediately feel comfortable while customizing their experience. Show that you care about them and satisfying their needs by asking meaningful questions. If you can, take the time to discover some of their personal interests, try to genuinely connect on a human level such as commenting about or acknowledging their interest or sharing your own experience with the shared interest. Perhaps the shared interest is sports, children etc. Remember the key is to be genuinely interested in them. The most successful sale people have a genuine interest in their client's well being and they show it. If you are not genuine, they will see through you from a mile away. If you have the luxury to prepare for a call on a specific prospect take time to research them so you know their interests or challenges before arriving.

   It took a little practice early in my sales career but whenever I walked into the office or home of a potential customer, I would observe the surroundings and look for clues such as pictures of sports teams, family or interesting items hanging on the wall and start a conversation about them. Learning about other people can be fun so have fun with it.

2. **Frame the Meeting.** With a great foundation of real trust established a great way to transition to the business portion of the meeting is to frame it. Before going any further take a minute to confirm the purpose of the meeting with the prospect. If your marketing message brought the prospect to you the next step is to find out why they agreed to meet, gauge their level of interest and where they are in the buying process. It should be clear to all that there will only be one of two outcomes. Either the prospect will decide that your product isn't right for them and will move on which is fine or you will both agree to take the next step in the process what ever that is. It is important to develop questions that will uncover the context of why they might buy your product. Why did they agree to meet with you or reach out? Some examples of questions you can ask or statements you can ask include:

"How did you find us and what prompted you to call/reach out/drop in?"

"What do you know about our product so far?"

"My goal for this meeting is to ensure that you have all the information you need to make a decision if my product is a fit for you. At the end of the meeting we will either agree that my product is not a fit for your we will agree to take the next step. Sound fair?"

Based on how the prospect answers these questions you are in a position to better understand their motivations which will help you to customize your presentation. It also confirms that it is worth everyone's time to continue. If a prospect mistakenly assumed that you can supply a product in 48 hours when it takes at least two weeks for delivery it might be a waste of time to continue. If they can accept a two-week delivery, then all is good. The last statement makes it clear that the purpose of the meeting is for them to acquire the information they need to be able to say "yes" or "no" to your product. If they are not willing to make a decision, you will have to decide whether to invest more time into the interaction or to respectively end the process.

3. **Discover Their Pain/Pleasure.** When a prospect responds to your marketing by reaching out or agrees to meet with you it is because there is something in your message that motivated them to act. The reason we buy anything is to either take away a pain or gain a pleasure. When we go to a restaurant, we are either taking the pain of hunger away or wanting to experience the pleasure of a great tasting dish and the social experience around it. Understanding what motivates a client to buy is crucial to a successful meeting. Remember that the perceived value of any product is directly related to the degree of pain removed or pleasure gained.

   If you had a minor headache you might ask me if I had a pain reliever with me. What if I said "Sure, that will be twenty dollars"? Your reaction might be, "thanks but if it costs twenty dollars I will live with the headache". Now, what if your headache was very painful to the point that you can barely function? Your reaction would probably be, "here is my twenty dollars". The fact is that the strength of the pain someone is feeling or the level of desire to feel pleasure will have a direct effect of their perceived value of the product and their willingness to pay a higher price.

   By fully understanding your prospects pains/pleasure points you will be able to customize your presentation and provide a meaningful presentation by knowing which features and benefits of your product will be most relevant to them while maximizing their perceived value of your product. Here is an example of a conversation between a sales person and the prospect if we were selling ¼" drill bits to a metal fabrication plant:

Sales Person: "What type of material you do typically drill now?"

Prospect: "½" steel"

Sales Person: "Wow, that's thick, how long does it currently take to drill a hole through that?"

Prospect: "about a minute"

Sales Person: "How many holes are drilled per day and what is your labour cost"?

Prospect: "500 holes per day and the labour cost is $200 total"

Sales Person: "Wow, that's about $50K per year ($200 x 250 days). How would it help your business if you could cut your labour cost in half?"

Prospect: "It would be huge, the $25K in savings would go directly to the bottom line and I could afford to buy that new truck"

Can you see what happened here? The sales person discovered that his product could save the prospect $25K per year. By asking what impact the savings would have on the prospects business the prospect started to feel the pain of paying $25K per year too much and started to feel the pleasure of buying that new truck. What do you think are the chances that the prospect will buy that drill bit? I'd be counting my sales commissions. Don't under estimate the power of a question. The only thing missing in this example is that we don't know how much the new drill bits cost vs the current one. As long as the additional cost of the new drill bits is less than $25K the client will get some value. If the total additional cost of the new drill bits is $5K then the client is saving 5X their investment, so it becomes a great move. The key is to position the price of your product against the perceived value to the customer so they can see the real benefit and will be happy to pay a higher price.

4. **Discover Their Budget.** Discussing money is awkward for a lot of people but if we want to be in business, we need to be able to talk about it openly. Having an idea of what your prospect is willing to pay will help you to recommend the right solution for them. I recently heard of a situation where a manufacturing client was willing to pay up to $30,000 to update some mechanical systems in their plant. Despite the manufacturer openly discussing this the plumbing company came in with a price of over $70,000. The manufacturer almost kicked the plumbing company's representative out of his office for wasting his time. The plumber wasted hours of his time producing the quote and the manufacturer was late starting the upgrade. There is nothing wrong with telling the customer that you can't help them if you know you can't provide a solution that at least is close to the client's budget.

5. **Decision Process.** Before investing bundles of time with a prospect be sure you are clear on their decision-making process. Is the person you are dealing with the actual decision maker? I have seen many sales people, including myself, who have a great sales meeting with the prospect to only find out at the close of the sale that the person needs to get further approval. This rarely works out because the person who was not at the meeting will only focus on the cost of your proposal without being aware of the benefits. I suggest to never allow someone else to do the selling for you. Try your best to have all decision makers at your sales meeting. If the client insists you only meet with the front-line person first, then make the goal of your meeting to earn the right to meet with the actual decision maker. If it is not possible to meet with the decision maker then provide a comprehensive proposal that provides all the details discussed in the meeting including the client's challenges, options, recommendation and benefits to the

client including a cost benefit analysis. Before investing further time to produce a proposal it is well within your right to gauge the prospect's level of interest. If you can't get a reasonable level of commitment from the prospect it might be time to walk away.

6. **The Presentation.** Once you have collected all the facts and understand the challenges and motivations of the prospect you are now ready to present your solution. Keep the content of your presentation specific to solving the pains and pleasures shared by the prospect and avoid talking about features and benefits that are not relevant to the prospect's situation. In the example of the sales interaction featured in Step 3 the sales person did a great job focusing on the speed and productivity of drilling through metal and how it would save the prospect thousands of dollars. How do you think the interaction would have gone if the sales person focused on the drill bit's ability to drill through any material without focusing on speed and cost savings? It is very likely the prospect would have written the drill bit off as the wrong solution and the sale would have been lost. We all get excited about our product and love to talk about it but how often do you think you lost a sale because you gave too much information that was not relevant to the prospect? It probably has happened more often than you think. Remember, when a prospect says, "thank you, let me get back to you" chances are you will not hear from them again.

7. **The Close.** This is the step in the sales process that causes many sales people to go into a cold sweat. Asking for the order and hearing "no" or other objections is terrifying for some. The sales process we are discussing in this chapter is designed to remove objections and move the prospect to a decision of "yes" or "no". You don't have to use all kinds of closing tricks or manipulation to get the order. Just ask for the order and they will buy if you were effective in the previous steps. It's really that simple. I recently had a client in a trades business who

used this process when quoting a job. Once he got to the close state he simply said, "If you would like to go ahead, I just need a 50% deposit to get you in the que". Without hesitation, the customer pulled out his credit card, handed it over and said," lets get it done". Yes, it really can be just that easy.

8. **Post Purchase Follow Up.** We are all subject to self doubt after we buy a product. The official term is *buyer's remorse*. What can you do to prevent "buyer's remorse" and avoid a possible cancellation or product return? Reinforce that they made the right decision in buying from you. This can include anything from sending an email or a card thanking prospect for the order to having someone from customer service follow up immediately to arrange delivery or set up the necessary appointments. This goes a long way to building a long-term sustainable relationship not to mention referrals to new clients.

Use *Figure 7.1* as your template and take yourself through this exercise to develop your own sales system. Find ways to continuously improve it and you will see amazing results very quickly. Remember, sales skills are like a golf swing, you never stop working on. If you feel you need help with your sales skills invest in yourself and take one of the many sales training programs available. There are numerous programs that range from a three-hour workshop to multiple weeks. Upgrading your sales skill or that of your sales team could be one of the best investments you make to grow your business.

Resist Price Discounting
Apples vs Oranges

How many times have you had a customer asked you to submit a proposal in a certain way so they could "compare apples to apples"? Of course, we take the path of least resistance by complying with the request. The customer does their comparison and then watches with joy as sales people from competing companies fight over their business and discount their prices as they chase each other to the bottom of the profit bucket. Don't let this happen to you.

So how do we break this pattern? How do we increase sales profitably? The secret is to resist the apples to apples scenario and convince the customer that oranges are better than apples. Focus on the specific features and benefits of your product and how it will solve problems better than other options. This requires more selling and convincing but if you follow the 8 Step Selling Process described in this book you will increase you chance of shutting out your competition and sell at a much higher margin not to mention avoiding jumping through hoops to get the order.

Early in my career I was selling security systems for a medium size alarm company. I was competing with 2 or 3 companies for almost every job. When you calculate the law of averages, I should have closed 25% – 33% of my quotes but I closed 80% over a 3-year period and my price was often 20% higher than most of the competition.

I didn't achieve this with my good looks. I designed security systems that were different than my competitors. I then convinced the customer that my design was the right one for them because it did a better job of protecting their family which was their priority and mine as well, since I truly cared about their safety. The prospects could not compare apples to apples so their decision criteria shifted from pricing to how well the family would be protected. My competitors were all selling apples and I sold oranges.

Selling oranges over apples often requires a paradigm shift from your customer. It takes an investment of more time and effort from yourself but if you are successful at changing the paradigm you will lock out your competition, increase sales conversions and sell for much higher margins.

Chapter 8

Increase Margins

Sharpen your pencil

In Chapter 5, I mentioned that I usually start with increasing gross profits when I work with a client to improve business performance because results can be achieved quickly. Your ability to maximize gross profits is key to driving the overall profitability of your business. Most business owners have complete control of their gross profits, yet they neglect to spend near enough time on improving it despite its importance to their business. This is mostly due to not knowing where and how to start the process or they are so busy fighting those daily fires that they don't have the time or energy to work on it. When we don't know how to start, we tend to procrastinate to the point that we either forget about it or just give up resulting in zero action taken.

Increasing gross margins can be achieved with two basic strategies that includes increasing prices and reducing Cost of Goods Sold (COGS). The rest of this chapter contains a step by step process on how to increase gross margins as well as some specific actions you can take to get you started.

Increase Prices

For many small and medium size business owners increasing prices is a nerve-racking endeavor. Whenever I suggest this to a client their response is, "my customers won't accept it, I will lose their business". I have analyzed many businesses that complain about poor cash flow and often found that they had not increased their price for years even though their own costs increased over the same time frame. When you have increasing costs combined with stagnate pricing gross margins will deteriorate very quickly resulting in poor cash flow.

I went through this exercise with a manufacturing client. They complained of poor cash flow, struggled to pay their bills and meet payroll and had no cash available to grow the business. After a review I discovered that they had not increased their price for four years while their COGS increased by two to three percent per year. I explained to my client that everyone expects annual inflationary increases just as he had accepted increases from his vendors. He agreed to implement a 4% price increase and emailed the notice to his customers that included an explanation that there had not been an increase for four years and he had to other choice but to increases prices. He waited nervously for their response, expecting the worst. Within twenty-four hours most of the customers responded with "thank you, I will update my records" and not one customer rejected the increase. My client was shocked by the nonchalant response of his customers and by how easy increasing pricing was to do. He is now a price increase Ninja, implementing price increases on a regular basis. His business has gone from struggling to break even to making over $300,000 in net profit every year.

Customers are much more likely to accept consistent nominal increases in short time intervals than large increases less often. For example, if you increase prices by 2.5% per year for four years you are likely to get much less push back than if you increased pricing by 10% every four years. If you were to increase pricing by 2.5% your profits will increase by $25,000 for each million dollars of sales. Imagine if you were to implement a 5% price increase, adding $50,000 of profit per million dollars of sales is a pretty good chunk of change for any small business owner.

Before implementing any price increase, be sure to benchmark your pricing against the competition. I am sure your business doesn't exist in a bubble, so you don't want to price yourself out of the market. However, this doesn't mean that you have to sell for the same price as your competition. Remember from our Chapters on Marketing and Sales that customers will pay more for a product if they can see how the perceived value will justify the higher price.

Resist Price Discounting

Have you ever been the buyer in a sales transaction and asked for a discount even when you already decided to go ahead just to see if you could get a better deal? What happened? Did the sales person cave and give you a discount or throw in "extras" as no charge? Think about it, you were willing to pay the stated price, and with the smallest amount of resistance the sales person folded like a deck of cards and discounted the product by 10% for no reason.

If the product was selling for $100 and it cost the company $60 the Gross Profit is $40. A $10 discount doesn't seem like much but in this case, it represents 25% of the Gross Profit ($10 discount/$40 gross profit). Most would agree that losing twenty five percent of gross profits is very significant and I would challenge any business to be viable losing twenty five percent of its gross profits.

If you find yourself or your sales team constantly discounting to "get the job" review the chapter on sales in this book or consider professional sales training. An untrained sales person will usually take the lowest path of resistance to make a sale. It's much easier for them to give a discount than taking the time to sell value. Learning to sell value vs. price can have a profound effect on your margins and profitability of your business. Make it painful for sales people to discount. Consider paying dramatically lower commissions or bonuses for sales that are below your listed price or if possible, have them get management approval for sales below a minimum margin level.

Challenge them when they ask for approval for a discount. Sales people are by nature very resourceful and will come up with some great reasons to discount such as "I need to discount to get the deal", "I will make more on the next sale" and so on. Instead of approving the discount coach them on how to sell the value. Discounting is occasionally needed but even if you can reduce unnecessary discounts by 50% your gross margins will dramatically increase, providing more cash to run your business. Let's use the above example where the sales person unnecessarily gave a 10% discount. If we could reduce overall discounting from 10% to 5% resulting in a 50% decrease in discounts the gross profit would increase by $5 from $30 to $35 or a 16% increase. Plug this into the magic profit formula and see what impact this would have on your net profits. Remember the magic profit formula requires us to increase gross profits by only 10% so we are already ahead of the game.

Surcharges & Ancillary Prices

Depending on your industry this type of revenue generators may already be accepted as the norm or looked at with distain by your customers. Tread carefully as you consider this option but if you can make it work your gross profits can increase beyond your wildest dreams. The types of charges I am talking about include fuel surcharges, shop fees, admin fees, etc. They usually appear at the bottom of the invoice and often annoy customers, but they usually just pay the bill and move on.

Many mobile businesses such as trucking companies, couriers, trades companies and even airlines charge a fuel surcharge that can range from a few percentage points to fifteen percent or more of the sale price added to the bill. I know of a mobile service company that struggled with fast rising fuel costs and decided to add a nominal 4%

fuel surcharge to each invoice. The extra revenue not only covered the increase in fuel costs it paid for all their fuel costs. It turned out to be a cash cow which is why you see so many companies doing it.

If you are not in a mobile business, consider adding shop charges if you are a manufacturing or logistics company. You could charge an environmental fee to cover costs of environmental compliances. Who can argue with saving the environment? If you do choose to add a surcharge be prepared to justify the fee to your customer when they ask about it. If it looks like a blatant cash grab your customers will resent it and you could lose their business. Keep in mind that there will always be customers that will not accept the additional fees, so you need to weigh the extra revenue against potential customer loss to ensure you are going to have an incremental improvement to gross profits.

The key is to not evaluate the surcharge just based on lost sales but consider its net impact on gross margins. For example, if your current sales are $1M and you add a 5% surcharge you will gain $50,000 in gross profit. If your gross margins are 40% and you loose $100,000 in sales because of the new charge the actual gross profit lost is $40,000 which means you are still ahead by $10,000 after implementing the charge. On the other hand, if the lost sales results in lost gross profits close to, equal or more than the net increase of gross profit the surcharge will create then it would not be a good idea to implement the surcharge.

When conducting your analysis come up with realistic best case and worse case scenarios to gauge the risk and then decide if you can live with the risk. Consider actions you can take to minimize the risk of lost sales such as a communication strategy to inform the customer ahead of time as well as how you will justify the charge. You may have to waive the charge for certain key customers if their push back is serious enough. Allow for a "slush fund" or budget for waived charges so you can forecast for the true effectiveness of the surcharge.

"Right Size" Your Labour Costs

The biggest "leak in the bucket" and drain on gross profits are unchecked labour costs. Most small business owners pay little attention to this except when they groan as they sign those payroll cheques. The profit drain is even more profound in industries where there is a high labour component in the product such as manufacturing, trades and construction, logistics and service companies.

I completely understand how difficult it is to make the harsh decisions that affect people's lives, but you need to decide on the purpose of your company. Is it to employ as many people as possible or is it to make a healthy profit so you can live a good living and live a legacy for your family? If your decision is that the purpose of your business is the former, then keep doing what you are doing. If it is the latter, then it's time to make some changes. Three areas you should focus on right now are (1) Benchmark labour costs against industry standards (2) Communicate productivity expectations to your team (3) Measure their results.

1. Benchmark Your Business

Every industry has benchmarks for the number of sales it requires to justify an employee. In the ivory towers of large corporations, the CEO will track the sales per Full Time Equivalent (FTE) to get a handle on whether current sales can support the size of the workforce. The FTE measurement is used to account for part time employees. If part time employees work twenty hours per week each would represent .5 of an FTE. A service company might use a metric of $150,000 of sales per FTE or a manufacturer might be $300,000 per FTE.

The sales per FTE measurement provides a good high-level indication if you are over staffed but it doesn't tell you what part of the business is overstaffed. Is it in production, management and administration or in sales? Every industry also has metrics for the number of people needed in each job type as a percentage of sales. Management, admin and sales costs are not typically included in cost of goods sold (COGS) so we will deal with them later. For now, let's focus on production labour.

Let's assume that your research shows that to be profitable your business needs a technician to generate about $1000 per day in revenue. If your daily service sales are $3000 and you have five technicians, you are only generating $600 per day per tech. If this is the case, I am willing to bet that your business isn't generating near the profits it should and you stress about cash flow. What would your profits look like if you ran the business with three techs at $1000 per day? Take one tech's annual wage burden and truck costs and multiply it by two. That's what will go right into your pocket! If in this case if you are not able to get the work done with three techs you likely have an issue with systems, productivity or motivation. Either way it comes down to your leadership and your level of attention to this key area of your business.

I worked with an HVAC company that increased their profits by $200,000 per year by making one simple adjustment to their business. They had eight techs despite industry metrics showing they should have only five techs. They right sized the business to five techs but struggled badly to complete the scheduled jobs on daily basis. After some review we found that techs were spending as much as two hours per day running to wholesalers to pick up items that they should have had in their trucks. Let's face it, when techs go to a wholesaler they don't just run in and out. They get a coffee and donut and catch up with buddies they run into while there. The solution was to establish a standard stocking list for trucks and delegate the responsibility to one of the office staff to ensure that all items needed for the scheduled jobs were in stock and on the truck. This reduced wasted time at the wholesaler by ninety percent resulting scheduled work being completed by five techs most of the time

Every industry has its own benchmark of what the percentage of the cost of goods (COGS) should be labour. If the labour percentage in your business exceeds industry norms, then it is likely that you are carrying more people than you need. I am sure you are asking where you can get this type of information? Here are a few suggestions: (1) Search online.

Try searching "sales per employee standards for (my) industry", "average sales per tech" or "percentage of labour costs for (my) industry." (2) Read trade journals or go to association websites for your industry. Many associations do surveys on benchmarking and publish the results, sometimes the reports are free but there is often a charge for it. Knowing the metrics for your industry is invaluable so seriously consider investing in the report (3) Ask your accountant or advisor. They will often have access to specialized reports or may already know the metric for your industry from experience.

2. Communicate Expectations to Your Team

Once you have established productivity standards for your team it is very important that they know what is expected of them. People will usually strive to meet your expectations but without expectations human nature is to work within our comfort zone which may not bring the results you need to generate a healthy profit.

I worked with a client in the transportation business that had been in business for several years. They were moderately profitable, but sales growth and profits had stagnated not to mention that the owner wanted to remove himself from the "engine room" of the business to take on higher value management tasks so he could accelerate the growth and profitability of the business

We realized very quickly that although the inside sales team was very dedicated, they were not given any targets to achieve. The client tracked overall performance of the team but not the performance of each team member. By using industry metrics and my client's experience we were able to establish productivity and performance standards for each team member, then we developed a system to track Key Productivity Indicators (KPIs) that would measure their performance. With our expectations and measurement system in place my client then clearly communicated his expectations to the team, challenged them to meet and exceed those expectations and rewarded them with a bonus system. This resulted in a lot of excitement and job satisfaction that propelled the company's growth for the next four years with sales doubling and profits increasing by 500% in that time.

3. Review Processes to Reduce Labour Waste

As mentioned earlier, labour is the single largest expense item in operations for many blue collar and service companies and is often the difference between generating a profit or loss and the quality of life the business owner will enjoy.

It is imperative that labour costs are tracked very closely. Without meaningful information it is impossible to make "informed" business decisions. Always remember, you can't manage what you don't measure.

The first step is to review all processes in each area of your business and look for unnecessary steps that slow down production without adding any value to the final outcome. I am reminded of a time when I was managing a plant with about eighteen production personnel. I stood in the plant one day and was observing how the raw material was being moved through the facility when I noticed that it was moved from one spot to the other to only to be moved again a short time later before being processed. I asked the shift supervisor why this was being done? His answer was, "That's the way we have always done it". I asked him to let me know what the impact would be if we removed that one step from the staging process and went direct to manufacturing.

A couple days later the shift supervisor came into my office with a bounce in his step and said enthusiastically, "We can reduce our labour cost by 30% without losing any throughput." I must be honest that I was shocked since I expected to save 10 – 15%. We implemented the change which did result in laying off people, but we increased gross profits by 30%. Remember, the purpose of the business is not to employee as many people as possible to make a profit so we can provide financial security for our family.

Here are a few tips to help you reduce labour costs.

1. Breakdown your processes into every single step, including even the smallest action. For each step ask yourself "What value does this step add to the process?" and "What would happen if we removed it?" Keep removing unnecessary steps until the operation is as lean as possible.

2. Be prepared to kill "sacrificial cows". Don't accept answers like "That's the way we have always done it". You will be amazed at how many people quietly questioned those long-standing methods but just didn't bother saying anything. Challenge your team and especially your management team to look for innovative ways to be more efficient and to share their ideas. Hopefully, you have created a culture that encourages innovation and openly sharing ideas. If this is not happening review the chapter in this book about building a winning culture.

3. Establish and communicate your expectations. As mentioned earlier in this chapter unless there are external expectations placed on us it is natural to work within our "comfort zone" that could leave a lot of potential not realized. By establishing productivity expectations, you will challenge your team to rise to the occasion and you may be pleasantly surprised by the results.

4. Get Out There! Do a ride along with your Techs or walk the shop floor. Keep an open mind. You may notice things that will shock and surprise you. While doing a ride along with a service driver I noticed that as he worked through the daily route he would crisscross down the street as they went from customer to customer on opposite sides of the street. Constantly crossing the street not only slowed his progress as he waited for traffic

to clear, it increased his chance of getting into an accident. We reorganized the route, so he visited all the customers on one side of the street and then visited the customers on the other side as he made his way back. Now instead of crossing the street multiple times per day he just had to make right turns. This not only improved productivity by thirty percent it was much safer for him and the public. It might help to have an outsider who has no biases or is affected by the outcomes to look at your business through a new set of lenses. They will often see things that you miss.

Running a business is like working on your golf swing or your slap shot in hockey. It will never be perfect but if you keep finding ways to improve your business just a little every day you will be able to look back and see the significant progress you have made.

The Profit is in The Soup

Do you remember the last time you went to a restaurant and the server had a soup of the day special? The featured soup is very often made from ingredients left over from the previous day's menu. The chef takes left over food that may have otherwise been thrown in the trash, makes a remarkable soup and then charges you handsomely for it. Since the Chef already costed the waste factor into the original menu item the soup is sold at or very near 100% profit.

Before the Chef relegates those left-over ingredients to the soup line, he first ensures that every ounce of the ingredient is used in the original menu item. Sides of meats and vegetables are cut to yield the highest volume of product. A loin of beef will be cut to generate eight portions instead of seven or a head of lettuce cut into six portions instead of five. Paying this amount of attention to waste can be the difference between profit and loss.

What are sources of waste in your business? A carpenter will have cut offs of lumber, an electrician will have roll ends of wire or a manufacturer will have "rejects" that don't pass quality tests or a waste bin full of unusable raw material. It is very much worth your time to spend time on this. Are your technicians or production staff taking due care to ensure you are maximizing raw material yields or are they literally throwing your profits out the door. Remember the story about the "rule of the hog" in Chapter 2 because you might have a leadership issue.

Assuming you have truly done everything you can to eliminate or at least minimize waste is there anything you can do with the waste by-product to generate extra income like the Chef does with soup? For example, can lumber cut offs be sold as fire wood? Can you sell end rolls of wire or piping through online platforms to the retail market or at least donate unusable product to non-profit organizations and get a tidy tax receipt? Be creative and bring others in to brain storm. They might see opportunities for by-product waste that you cannot see.

If waste is unavoidable be sure to measure and track waste levels and build it into your Cost of Goods Sold (COGS). I know of a manufacturing company that estimated their waste factor to be 30% and built it into their costs. After conducting a study where we measured waste levels for a few batches of product, we found the actual waste factor to be 40%. Since product mark ups were based on a cost assuming a 30% waste factor instead of 40% the actual COGS was much higher than estimated meaning gross profits were much lower than it should have been. Prices were adjusted to reflect the true cost to produce the product and gross profits immediately increased by over 25% translating into hundreds of thousands of dollars per year in new profits and cash flow. I will talk more about measuring waste in Chapter 9 when I will cover Key Productivity Indicators (KPIs).

Account for Every Component of Your Product

It doesn't seem to matter the industry when I review product costs with business owners and question how they account for minor components of their product their response is "Oh, we just include it as a value add". When I ask to see the cost accounting to confirm that they included the item in their product cost they are almost never able to show me that the item was in fact accounted for.

Low cost items might seem incidental, but your business could die a death of a thousand cuts from the little things adding up over time. Some examples of inaccurate costing include a food manufacturer who put sticky labels on their package to emphasize freshness but didn't include it or the labour to attach it in their product cost. There are trucking companies who didn't charge a fuel surcharge which is a normal industry practice or plumbing and electrical contractors that don't account for the cost of connectors, solder or even set up time in their costs.

In the case of the food manufacturer the total cost of applying the label was only $.03 per unit but when your cost to produce is $1.00 the hit on gross margins is 3%. This goes a long way to improving gross profits by ten percent in our Magic Profit Formula.

The trucking company was losing ten percent of its gross profits by not accounting for fuel costs and the electrical and plumber contractors were losing as much as three percent by not costing their roll ends and cut offs. Now three percent doesn't sound like much, but it translates to $30,000 for every $1M of sales. I challenge you to show me someone who wouldn't mind an extra $30,000 in their pocket.

Follow these steps to calculate accurate costs of your product

1. Use a chart like the one shown in Fig *8.1* and <u>itemize every single</u> component of your product. This includes every connector, product label, box, master pack, shipping label, everything!

Try reverse engineering by disassembling a completed product ready for shipping one piece at a time while recording each item.

2. Utilize your purchase records to determine the actual cost and quantity of the item in the product and extend the price for total cost.

3. Know your real cost of labour. Just as you did with the component, itemize each type of labour such as design and assembly plus the amount of time needed for every single step of the process. Determine the cost of the labour and record it in the appropriate column. Let's say your total labour burden is $20/hr and the employee can complete the step of the process in one minute or less. This means that the employee can process 60 items per hour. If we divide the $20/hr by 60 units, the total labour cost is $0.33 per unit. Remember to account for set up time in your labour calculation. In trades business, be sure to factor in set up and clean up times as well as production time into your labour costs. Transportation companies will need to account for wait times or traffic conditions and warehouse operations will have to account for time for the picker to get to right location of the product as well as the time to actually pick it.

4. With all columns completed, extend pricing and add up the total.

How does this compare to what you thought your cost was? My guess is that you were unpleasantly surprised. Well, at least you now know the truth and can make the necessary adjustments.

Fig 8.1

Product Cost Sheet			
Product:		Batch:	Date:
Raw Material	Units	Cost/Unit	Total
Item 1			
Item 2			
Item 3			
Item 4			
Total Raw Material			
Labour	Units	Cost/Unit	Total
Stage 1			
Stage 2			
Stage 3			
Total Labor			
Supplies	Units	Cost/Unit	Total
Item 1			
Item 2			
Total Supplies			
Packaging	Units	Cost/Unit	Total
Item 1			
Item 2			
Item 3			
Total Packaging			
Misc	Units	Cost/Unit	Total
Item 1			
Item 4			
Total Misc			
Total All Sections			

Ask Suppliers for Lower Pricing

This might seem obvious and very simple but when was the last time you asked a supplier for lower pricing? How often are you asked by your customers to lower your price and then comply to "keep the business". I'm not aware of very many situations where a supplier approached a customer and said this is your lucky day, I am lowering your price by 5%. On the other hand, I have seen a pretty good batting average of suppliers lowering their price when asked.

The price you negotiated a couple years ago might have been fair then but if your purchases grew as your sales grew you will likely qualify for a better volume discount. If you currently spread your business evenly between three suppliers, it might be worth approaching your favorite supplier and negotiating better pricing by promising to give them half or more of your business. Also consider ordering common high-volume items in large quantities if your cash flow can handle it. Discounts can be very substantial when buying cases or pallets at a time instead of individual packages and have a significant impact on your margins.

When I was in a supplier role throughout my own management career my motto was "volume talks, give me the volume and I will give you better pricing". This response worked more often than not and the customer would increase their purchases with me. Although I gave up some profit margin sales increased so much that I ended up making much more profit dollars than before the discount.

Section III

Manage Like a CEO

Chapter 9

Stop Using Beer Case Metrics

Be thirsty for numbers

Many business owners anxiously await the release of their financial statements so they can see how their business did. At best the financials are reviewed monthly but more often than not they get reviewed on an annual basis.

How do business owners measure their performance in the meantime, so they know how they are doing now? Unfortunately, many use the "Beer Case" method of measuring performance. Think about a typical business week. You work yourself to the bone putting in a ridiculous number of stressful hours. On Friday afternoon you rush to the bank, deposit all the cheques and cash that came in by noon and then head back to the office as quick as you can to pay your staff and suppliers and maybe even yourself if you are lucky. After all this, if there is still enough money left over to treat yourself to a case of beer you must be doing OK. In other words, you have no true measurement system and don't have a clue about how you are really doing.

When they do review their financials, the two numbers that the business owner looks at are top line revenue and the big number at the bottom, profit/loss. If the numbers are less than expected how do you make decisions on which corrective actions to take? By the time you get the financial statements a lot of water has flowed under the bridge and many opportunities to improve business performance have passed by or have continued to cost you a lot of money. By not measuring key parts of the business on a daily, weekly and monthly basis it is almost impossible to understand what caused the low performance? Was it sales, profit margins or productivity? Where and how do you even start to investigate the story behind the numbers?

Consider the amount of activity that is happening under the hood of your vehicle as you drive through town. There are crankshafts and pistons moving, explosions happening, electronic pulses and fluids being pumped all at the same time. How do you know if everything is OK with the engine? I suppose you can listen for weird noises but by the time those appear it could be too late; the damage is probably already done. Ideally it is best to take care of the problem before you can hear it. How do you do this? You probably look at the dash board.

By monitoring about 5 different activities in the engine such as speed, RPMs, temperature, oil pressure and battery voltage you have a very good idea if your engine is running smoothly and where to look if there is a hiccup. If the oil pressure is low, you might be low on oil or have an issue with the oil pump. If battery voltage is low, you might have a problem with the alternator, or the battery needs replacing. The dashboard tells you that you have a problem and what could be causing it so you can investigate further and deal with the problem before your engine blows up or stalls on the side of the road.

By creating a dash board of your business and measuring Key Productivity Indicators (KPIs) you will be able to monitor the performance of your company on a daily or weekly basis and take corrective action in real time rather than waiting weeks or months to get the information you need. A good KPI tracking system can tell you whether you are on track to meet your profit goals for the financial period even when you are still in middle of the period. For example, if you generate financial statements on a monthly basis, a KPI system will let you know on a weekly basis if you are on track to meet your profit goals.

In Chapter 8, I spoke about how a transportation company used KPIs to more than double their sales and increase profits by 500% in four years. Although the team rose to the challenge, we were also able to identify bottle necks in the sales conversion process by determining which sales people were meeting and exceeding expectations and those who were not meeting expectations. Based on feedback from the struggling sales person we provided additional training and mentorship until they either met expectations or it was determined that the position just wasn't right for them.

The amount of activity you need to monitor will depend on the complexity of your business. It is recommended to identify at least five key areas of your business you can monitor to ensure that your business is performing as expected.

Our natural reaction is to measure sales and gross margins which are important, but it is equally to measure the non-financial activities that lead to the financial performance. For example, if you are in the manufacturing business look at the units /hour produced. In the trades you might want to measure billable hours per day per tech. The chart shown in *Fig 9.1* provides some ideas on what you could measure based on your business sector. By establishing the number of units per hour that is required to generate a desired gross profit you can monitor this metric daily to ensure your unit/s per hour on track. If they are not you can investigate and take corrective action quickly instead of waiting for your next financial statements to come out.

Fig 9.1

Common KPIs by Sector			
Mobile Trades	Manufacturers	Contractors	Logistics
• Revenue per day per tech • % of Callbacks • Service calls per day per tech • Average revenue per call per tech • Product sales per tech • % of payroll on injured status • % of overtime of total payroll • Vehicle operating cost by hour	• Units produced per hour by station • Waste factor % • Order turnaround time • Defect rate % • Set up time per day • Equipment downtime (% of hours) • Injuries % of payroll on injured status	• Billable hours per man per day • Units installed per hour/day (length, items, volume etc.) • Injuries % of payroll on injured status • Labor vs budget • Materials vs budget	• Orders shipped per day • Avg pieces per order • Pick time per order • Order turnaround time • Pieces picked per day/hour • Pallets shipped per day • Container load/ unload time (manhours) • Injuries % of payroll on injured status

A common KPI in the trades is to measure the number of billable hours per day. As an indication of the tech's productivity you can set daily goals for billable hours that would roll up to achieving weekly and monthly service revenues. If the number of billable hours is below the target amount, you at least know where to investigate and can take immediate corrective action to nip any problems in the bud. An HVAC client used this exact metric to solve an issue with a tech whose daily revenue was less than the other techs. The billable hours per day of the tech in question was six hours when the billable hours per day for all the other techs ranged from eight to ten hours. With this discover the owner investigated and found that the tech was underbilling customers. The labour rate was $150 for the first hour and $95 per hour after. If the tech was on site for 1.5 hours, he would only charge the $150 first hour charge because there was no partial hour pricing and he didn't' feel right charging the customer for a full hour. The owner adjusted the price schedule and created a $55 charge for one half hour. The tech used this pricing and increased his billable hours six to eight hours per day with his overall revenue increasing by twenty five percent.

The KPIs listed in the chart are meant to give you an idea of what can be tracked. If you don't see your business sector or other KPI items in the chart, ask others in your industry about what they track. Suppliers are a good source of information since they usually have a very good overview about how the industry does things. Also consider asking your accountant or a consultant for direction.

Tracking Data

Once you have determined what KPIs you need to track for your business the next step is to decide what data you need to collect to build your reports and how you will collect it. By now you must be thinking that it would be great to have all this information but where does it come from? It's simple, the raw data comes from your techs or foremen in the field if you are in the trades or mobile service business or the shop floor or drivers if you are in the manufacturing or logistics business.

Having an effective data collection system requires structure and discipline. Structure is needed so that everyone understands their role in collecting the data and how they will do it. Discipline is needed to ensure that the data is collected the same way, every time, by everybody. Without discipline data collection will be sporadic resulting in unreliable reports and undermining the whole KPI system.

There are two ways to collect data from the front lines: (1) Paper forms (2) Electronic forms. Paper forms can be a good way to get started in the KPI game. They are relatively easy to design and can be produced quickly to get you started right away. In the case of a mobile service business much of the information can be gathered from the work order. Items such as time on job, travel time, labour revenue and product revenue can be collected. If your techs are not currently recording the information you need then either redesign the form or have them enter the information in unused space.

In stationary businesses such as manufacturing, production staff would fill out a form for their own workstation. Depending on the data you need to collect they might have to record the batch number or product they worked on and the time spent working on it. If there is a waste factor, they could record all the raw material entering their station and the amount of finished material leaving it.

In both cases someone must be responsible for entering the information from the forms onto a spreadsheet that has been formulated to tally all the information and produce the KPI information you require. Paper collection can work well but the downside is that it requires the additional step and time of someone manually entering all the data. It is also important that a check and balance be in place to ensure that all paperwork is completed properly and gets handed in. Otherwise you risk having the forms and their valuable information being lost forever.

Electronic data collection is more complex to set up and often comes with a cost to set it up and to run it. The advantage is that the process is streamlined and eliminates the shortcomings of paper such as manually entering information onto a spreadsheet or losing the paperwork. With electronic collection, devices such as laptops, tablets or even smartphones are provided to the techs or workstations. As they enter the information into the electronic form the data can be automatically rolled into a report in real time. This means getting the information faster and eliminating the additional step of manually entering information onto a spreadsheet. Electronic collection systems can range from the front-line staff entering their information directly onto a spreadsheet that sits in a shared folder you can easily access to an electronic platform such as manufacturing software or apps for mobile businesses. There are many of these products in the market place and can be easily found with an online search.

Starting with paper forms and a spread sheet is a good way to get started if you are new to the KPI game. It allows time for the KPI culture to be entrenched into your business as everyone gets comfortable with the discipline of collection. It also allows you to easily fine tune the type of information you need to collect by adjusting the forms. You can upgrade to an electronic system once you have solidified your KPI process.

Stop using beer case metrics to run your business. If you instill measurement tools into your business, you will not only be able to afford that case of beer on Friday you will know exactly how many cases you can afford weeks in advance.

Chapter 10

Cash is King

Where is my money??

We have all heard the term "cash is king" but we usually don't hear anyone saying that "sales is king" and for very good reason. The fact is that we can make all the sales in the world but if we don't have the cash on hand today to pay our suppliers or make payroll they will stop selling us product, employees will stop working and the government might seize your account if you can't pay your tax bill. Many profitable and viable companies have been shut down due to lack of cash.

You can try to hold off suppliers for payment for a short amount of time but if you can't make payroll your employees are likely going to walk away and shut down your business. It is likely that you struggle with cash flow because the business just isn't profitable due to so many leaks in the bucket that your sales just can't keep up with the out flow of cash. On the other hand, many profitable companies struggle with cash flow due to several other reasons that can be easily fixed. The most common reason is that they don't manage the "cash gap".

Fig 10.1

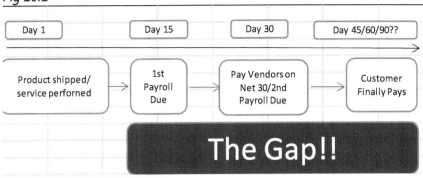

Manage the "Cash Gap"

The "cash gap" is that period that lies between you getting paid and your obligation to pay your bills on time. In *Figure 10.1* you can see how the cycle starts with the delivery of your product or completion of your service. You send the invoice and hope you are paid in 30 days because in the meantime you have a cash gap because you have payroll in 15 days, another payroll in 30 days plus your suppliers want to be paid in 30 days. Many businesses can get through the first 15 days but if your customers don't pay you on time you now have a serious cash gap. Here are a couple causes of a cash gap and how to prevent it.

A/R Days – Many business owners are so caught up on the "fun" stuff like sales and marketing or creating products that they pay little attention to Accounts Receivable. They wait until they are so strapped for cash that they risk not making payroll the next day. They finally say, "Hey, I wonder who still owes me money" and then prints the A/R Ageing Report. Upon review they find that many customers are 10, 20, 30, 45 or more days past due with amounts totaling tens of thousands of dollars and then wonder why they can't meet payroll. They get on the phone and start calling customers in desperation to get money fast resorting to giving discounts if the customer pays now. The problem is that you just unnecessarily gave up profits not to mention you taught your customer if they hold on to your money long enough, they can get a better deal from you. So much for trying to increase profits. Also think about the message you are conveying. If you show desperation to your customers, you risk losing their confidence and their business

It is imperative that we monitor the "Age" of our receivables weekly or on a monthly basis at the very least. Make it a habit to review you're A/R Ageing Report every week and mark it in your calendar to make sure you don't forget. If your terms are Net 30 Days contact every account that is over 30 days even if they are one day overdue. When I was a branch manager for a distribution company, I was having lunch with a client who was in our top 20 list for purchases but was notorious for paying in 45 to 60 days when our terms were Net 30. In a moment of weakness, he let it slip that his company didn't pay bills until they got a call from the vendor. In other words, he was using his supplier's money as a line of credit instead of paying interest to the bank. I took note of this and instructed my A/R person to call the customer right at the 30-day mark. It worked!! We started getting paid in about 35 days. Getting paid 10 to 15 days earlier represents a whole payroll cycle and can be the difference whether you make your next payroll.

In a perfect world everyone will pay their bills right at 30 days. The fact is that there will always be some that pay in 40 day and even 60+ days. A couple key numbers to look at on the A/R report are the *average days* and the *percentage of A/R dollars that is over 60 days*. The average days will give you immediate feedback on the general state of your accounts receivable. Typically, if your average days is within five days of your payment terms you have an effective A/R management system. For example, if your terms are Net 30 you want to see the average days to be under thirty-five. On the other end of the spectrum avoid having more than ten percent of your total A/R over 60 days and in some industries the number is 45 days. Once an account gets to this level the risk of it becoming delinquent increases dramatically. The key is prevention. Get on them early and be prepared to put their credit on hold if needed. The sale is not complete until the cheque is deposited and cleared by the bank.

One strategy to prevent accounts for going over acceptable payment times is to have a structured follow up system that escalates with each step. The following is an example of an account receivable acceleration program assuming a Net 30 payment term.

1. At 30 days send a friendly note to remind the customer that the invoice is now due and to please let you know if they haven't received the invoice. At this step you are the nice guy and are avoiding blaming them by implying that they might have not received the invoice

2. At 40 days make a friendly phone call to ask when you can expect payment. If they give a date thank them and let them know you will look forward to receiving it. If the cheque doesn't arrive on the stated date, then call immediately to let them know you have not received the cheque. If the customer claims that the cheque was sent, then ask for cheque number and date sent. If they don't fulfill their obligation to send the cheque as promised you will then have to consider putting them on credit hold and let them know by letter.

3. The key is persistence. Keep calling. The squeaky wheel gets the grease. Be very squeaky and it is likely you will be paid.

4. Once the account reaches 60 days and you do not feel comfortable with the customer's response or have serious doubts about getting paid it might be time to send them to collections. Send them a stern warning letter about this and find a good collections company if payment isn't made in the very near future.

Invoicing Cycle – It's one of the easiest things to fix and can be a major factor whether you make payroll or not, yet many business owners pay much too little attention to their billing cycle. It is imperative that you get the invoice for your goods and services to your customer immediately upon completion of the transaction. A delay of a few days might not seem like much but when it's the day before payroll and you don't have the cash to make it, expecting the money in a few days won't help you make it tomorrow. The faster you get the invoice out the faster the money will come in. Customers often pay invoices based on the time they receive it so if you wait two weeks to send it and have terms of Net 30 you will not be paid for at least 6 weeks assuming the customer actually pays 30 days from receipt of the invoice. This means that you have to carry your company's operating expenses for 6 weeks! That's a lot of money needed in the bank just to survive.

In a typical mobile service business. the technician will hit the road with workorders for the day. They go about their work and as the calls pile up, they lose track of their paper work. When the day is over, the tech returns to the office and hands in the completed workorders to be invoiced. What nobody is aware of is that two workorders fell between the seats and sat there undetected for two weeks before the tech finds them by accident. He takes them into the office soiled with coffee stains and with his tail between his legs he hands them in to the bookkeeper. Darn, the owner sure could have used the money from those invoices to make payroll last week. If you are in the trades, I am sure this has happened to you more than once. I see it all the time when I review businesses.

In the manufacturing industry there are often delays in sending the invoice because someone is waiting for a production report, a bill of lading or the invoice sits on the receptionist's desk for a few days waiting to be mailed. Remember, a few days can determine if you make payroll in a few weeks.

Getting invoices in customers' hands as fast as possible needs to be your top priority. Review your paper flow and see how you can shorten the cycle. Be sure your employees understand the importance of getting invoices out quickly, so the receptionist doesn't wait three days to mail them. If you still use a paper system, then have a control system in place to ensure that every workorder that leaves the office comes back and assign the responsibility to someone to make sure it happens. Make it a policy for foremen to get time sheets and other reports to the office immediately or for the warehouse to confirm right away, that the order was shipped so the invoice can be sent.

If you are still using paper-based systems for workorders and reports, consider switching to a digital platform. There are numerous affordable cloud based and offline platforms that allow mobile techs, foremen and remote locations to submit their reports electronically in real time from a tablet, phone or laptop so you have instant updates of workorders and shipping information. No more delays in invoicing because workorders fell between seats not to mention that many of these platforms can provide detailed operation and sales information that will help you run your business more efficiently.

Lack of Planning – There an old saying, "If I knew you were coming, I would have baked a cake", that people would use when someone unexpectedly showed up to their home for a visit. In other words, if the host knew the visitor was coming over, they would have been better prepared. A cash flow crunch is like that unexpected visitor where we don't see it coming until it arrives, then we scramble to deal with it.

Wouldn't it be nice if we could predict when and if a cash flow crunch would arrive? Well, it is possible to predict it with enough accuracy that you can dramatically reduce or even eliminate unexpected crunches. Every business should conduct a cash flow analysis. A cash flow analysis is like a budget where you forecast sales, expenses and profits to see how much you will make. The difference is that a cash flow analysis doesn't predict when the revenue or expenses will be incurred but when the money from those transactions will come in and out of your bank account. For example, a budget might show sales of $100,000 in January but the cash flow analysis will show the $100,000 coming into the business in February if terms are Net30. If your customers pay at time of service then it is OK to show the cash coming in the same month as the transaction.

With a cash flow analysis expenses need to be accounted for when they are paid instead of when they are incurred. For example, if your insurance is $12,000 per year your accountant might show it as $1000 per month on your profit and loss statement but the actual invoice is paid at the beginning of the year. Whereas the profit and loss statement will show the $1000 per month expense a cash flow analysis will show the whole $12000 in the month that the bill is due to be paid.

Predicting when a cash flow crunch might occur and how severe it will be, allows us to prepare for the "crunch" or even prevent it all together. By predicting cash short falls ahead of time, you can make financing arrangements well in advance with your bank which is much healthier than trying to secure funding when behind the "8 ball". Banks get very nervous when customers arrive desperate for financing as it might indicate mismanagement and a high risk for delinquency

I went through this exercise with a client that was growing very quickly. Sales tended to peak from March to October with lower sales from November to February. Terms were Net 30 but A/R days were at 37 days. Since his company was expected to pay their bills within 30 days, we had to be sure that there was adequate cash available to cover the 7-day gap between paying bills and receiving money from customers. There were also months that had higher than usual expenses such as a large annual insurance premium. When we completed the cash flow analysis, we found that he would be about $50,000 short of cash two months of the year due to high bills and lower sales with the first crunch coming in about 3 months. He went to his bank and arranged a line of credit to cover the cash flow gap. When the expected cash short fall arrived as expected he had the resources available to cover it and we avoided a lot of stress and anguish.

When conducting a cash flow analysis be sure to include expenditures that are not expenses such as capital purchases. If you are planning to buy machinery or a truck with cash include the require cash outlay in your analysis so you can predict a possible crunch. If you can, try to avoid the crunch by holding off major expenditures to months when more cash is available or propose a payment plan to your vendor that will fit within your cash flow capabilities.

"Just in Case" Management- The one common phrase I hear from business owners who struggle with cash flow and profitability is "just in case". When I conduct a financial review of manufacturers, distributors, trades and logistics businesses I often find they have too many employees or carry as much as 50% to 100% more inventory than needed.

It doesn't seem to matter the type of business I am reviewing but when I tour the stock room with the owner we often find stock levels of many items to be at disproportional levels in relation to sales for that item or there is stale inventory with an inch of dust on products from sitting on the shelve for months or even years. In either case both results in low inventory turns. When I ask why they carry so many low volume or old items the answer is usually "just in case" someone needs it.

I get the same answer when its discovered that they have too many employees for their level of sales. "Just in case it gets busy or someone calls in sick." I understand that it is hard to let people go. We all want to hope that things will get better so we won't have to let anyone go. The fact is that carrying too many people drains your profits, drains your cashflow and can put your company at risk for failure, not to mention it can place your family and all your employees in peril. Remember, the role of your business is to make money and build value for the future, not to employee as many people as possible.

As these business owners hold on to their "just in case" philosophy of running their business they struggle to meet payroll, pay their suppliers, or can't grow due to a lack of funds. During times of increasing interest rates, it is important to pay attention to your inventory levels. The double-digit interest rates of the late 70's and early 80's taught business the real cost of carrying too much inventory. The carrying charges alone had a dramatic effect on COGS, causing many companies to struggle or go out of business. For example, if your average inventory is $100,000 and you are paying .5% interest per month it will cost you $500 per month to carry the inventory which is added directly to your COGS. If interest rates were to increase to 1.5% per month like they did many years ago your carrying charges would increase to $1500 per month. If the inventory takes three months to turn over your carrying costs are now $4500 (3 months x $1500). When you think about it your gross margins just decreased by 4.5% which is a big leak in the bucket.

I suggest applying the "80/20 rule" to inventory management. In almost every case 20% of the SKUs produce 80% of the revenue. Conversely, this means that 80% of the SKUs are producing only 20% of the sales. This is a significant amount of money to tie up for the occasional sale. If part of your value proposition is to have slow moving items on hand as a convenience for your customers, then the margins should be higher. It is often more feasible to bring in these low selling items on an "as need basis" with the understanding that you will make less margin. The benefit is that you will free up cash to grow your business instead of tying it up on slow moving items that produce little profit.

Instead of "Just in Case" inventory management try to adopt a "Just in Time" philosophy. In a perfect world, new items will come in the back door just as old items are sold out the front door. The key is to find a balance between having enough inventory, so you don't run out but to also not sit on more inventory than needed. Adopting a min/max system that is constantly updated will help to keep inventory at optimal levels, so your cash is not sitting idle and giving you the flexibility to grow or reward yourself for the fruits of your labour.

Chapter 11

You Might Not Be as Rich as You Think

Warning: you could be running a "fixer upper"

Business owners are some of the most inspiring people on earth. I am inspired by their hard work, perseverance through adversity and dedication and commitment to making a difference in their industry and community. If all goes right, they get to make a great living so they can support their family and have some profit left over to enjoy some of the good things in life.

However, despite the owner's hard work and dedication running a successful and profitable business there are many well established businesses that do not create the level of wealth needed to fund the owner's retirement so they can live the life they had always dreamed. Instead of taking that trip around the world they live with staycations or they can't buy that car or truck they had always wanted.

It is true that producing great products and services while making a profit helps build business value and wealth but there are several factors that many business owners do not consider that can have a profound effect on business value and the lifestyle you can expect in life after business.

Building value in a business is very much like building equity in your home. We update our kitchens and bathrooms, install hardwood floors and put on a fresh coat of paint so we can feel good about our home. The bonus is that updating our home will also increase the value in case we ever want to sell it. Your business is no different. It is equally important to maintain and update your business, so your equity continues to grow and provide the maximum payoff when you are ready to cash out.

How a Buyer Values Your Business

Business Valuators use many methods to determine business value. They will often use three to five methods on one valuation to see how the numbers work out. If all goes well the results of each method will be similar so coming up with the final number is straight forward. If the result of the methods used are significantly different the valuator will triangulate the numbers and then use their own judgement and experience to come up with the final valuation. Two common methods used are *owner's cash flow* and *a multiple of profits*.

Owner's cash flow includes all items the ownership draws from the business. This includes typical items such as salary and profits but can also include "discretionary" items such as the owners paying themselves above market value for the job they have in the business, above average company vehicle allowances or memberships to exclusive clubs. There is no set multiplier for determining value based on owner's cash flow as there are a number of factors involved but a multiplier somewhere around 2.5X is often used.

A second method of valuation that is very popular is to apply a multiple of net profits. The multiplier can range greatly from less than 1X to well over 5X of annual profits depending on the industry and current state of the business but a 4X to 5X multiplier of profits is often considered to be a desirable number.

To have a true sense of the real profits the financial statements need to be "normalized". This is a process where your discretionary cash flow is separated from the regular business expenses so that a buyer can more accurately determine the true profitability of the business if they were to run it themselves. Discretionary items are expenses or cash withdrawals that the owner chooses to put through the business that would not necessarily be considered normal expenses or chosen by another owner. Some items that will typically be reviewed are:

1. Is the owner paying himself or family members market rate wages based on the job they have in the business? Market rate wages refers to what they would have to pay someone else to do the job if the owner wasn't there. If the owner pays himself over market value, then the amount over the market rate will be added back to profits. If the amount is under market value the difference between market value and the actual value will be added to expenses thus reducing the actual profits. I have seen business owners purposely pay themselves under market value in the years leading up to selling the business to make the profits look better than they really are. A good valuator should be able to detect this.

2. Does the business lease or own company vehicles used by family members or does the owner drive an expensive vehicle that isn't really required for the business? This is an expense that a new owner might choose not to continue which would increase profits.

3. Is the rent at market value? There are situations where the business rents its premises from a related company owned by the same person and pays an amount either well above or below market value. I won't get into all the reasons why this would be done but there are several strategies involving taxation and estate planning involved in this strategy. The point is to always verify that the rent paid reflects current market conditions or you could be in for a big surprise at renewal time.

Keep in mind that there are many other factors that can affect business value such as competitive position, growth trends, intellectual property and management competence. Value can also be affected by whether the buyer will "roll-in" the operations of the purchased company into their current operations or if the business will be bought as a "going concern" and continue in the current format. A roll-in is when the purchased company is absorbed into the buyer's operations where the two parties will literally move in together under one roof and operate on one system. When a business is purchased as a going concern the business being purchase continues to run as a separate entity under its own roof and operating platform. In other words, it's basically business as usual with only ownership changing.

Three Stages of Business Value

Similar to a home, when buying a business a buyer not only looks at the profits but at a number of other key factors to determine if your business falls into one of three categories: (1) Fixer Upper (2) Fair Market Value (3) Strategic Buy. Which category does your business fit into?

Fixer Upper – Businesses in this category are not necessarily losing money. In fact they could actually be making a very good profit. It is usually during the due diligence process when the buyer gets to look under the hood of the business, they discover that significant investments in time & money would have to be made to update systems, invest in new equipment or replace people who were not productive or even competent. This business is often sold for much less than Fair Market Value.

To use the buying a house analogy, despite the house being structurally sound, the new owner would have to repaint walls that had not repainted for 20 years, update that 1970's kitchen and bathroom and do some major landscaping to improve curb appeal. Before a buyer could buy the house, they would need to estimate the amount of money needed to bring the house up to their desired standards and then discount the price enough to make it worth their effort which is often much more than the amount needed to invest. For example, it if was determined that they needed to invest $50K to upgrade the property they might want a discount of $75K to $100K. The same concept can be applied to a business. If a buyer determines that they need to invest an additional $100K in a new computer system and a forklift, not to mention committing their own efforts to streamline operations, they would likely expect a discount of $150K to $200K or more to compensate them for their time and efforts. You will need to decide whether to make the investments yourself and reap the benefits later or sell the business "as is" and accept the much lower amount.

Fair Market Value – Imagine driving up to a home that you were thinking of buying and seeing well-groomed landscaping and fresh coat of paint on the exterior of the house. Once inside, you immediately notice new hardwood floors, fresh interior paint and beautiful plumbing fixtures in the kitchen and bathrooms. There is no further investment for you to make to update the home. It is very likely that you would be willing to pay the asking price for the house because you appreciate the work that was already put into the home and value the convenience of just having to turn the key and move in.

Like the home described above, a business that has up to date systems and procedures in place, well maintained equipment and quality staff will likely be sold for fair market value. This means that the selling price will be in line with what other well-run businesses in that industry are currently being sold for.

Strategic Buy – To continue with our home buying analogy, would you be willing pay more for a home if it had unique features not normally found in a home in the area or price range? Perhaps it has beautiful archways, meticulously crafted woodwork or a man cave with all the amenities like wet bar, pool table, big screen TV and lounging chairs with cup holders. If finding all of these features in a house was very rare it is very likely that you would pay more than asking price especially if other buyers were submitting offers. The same can be applied to businesses. It is possible for a business to be sold for above fair market value if it has specific unique attributes that are attractive to potential buyers. It could have a much sought-after brand or great reputation in the market place. It might have proprietary processes or hold patents on key technology. It could also be as simple as having a product line or a customer base that would integrate wonderfully with the buyer's business and increase its profits.

There is that old saying that "beauty is in the eyes of the beholder". This is just as true when a buyer is considering the purchase of the business. The amount of premium he is willing to pay is based on how bad he wants it. If the business possesses those unique features that he greatly values or if other buyers are in pursuit, he is much more likely to pay the premium. Does your business offer any features or attributes that others would place a high value on?

8 Signs That Your Business Could be a Fixer Upper

There was a TV commercial by a company that was promoting reverse home mortgages for baby boomers who needed cash but wanted to stay in their home. As the commercial begins the husband says, "We don't want to move, we love every outdated nook and cranny in our home". Our homes are very personal with many memories contained within. It is the same for business owners. I am sure you built your business with sweat and blood and many sleepless nights so the last thing you need is to be insulted by someone telling you that "your business is a fixer upper".

Hopefully your business is not a fixer upper and falls into the *fair market value* or *strategic buy* categories but what if it is a fixer upper? Let's confirm it right here, right now. The following are eight signs that your business could be a fixer upper. As you read each statement be honest with yourself as you either agree or disagree with each statement.

1.   Profits Margins are Below Average for My Industry
We spoke about benchmarking earlier in this book to confirm if your company's performance was less than, equal or better than others in

your industry. The bottom line is the bottom line here. If your gross profit margin and/or your net profit margin is below the industry average a buyer will consider this to be a red flag and will immediately consider your business to be a fixer upper because they will need to invest time and money to improve margins.

2. Sales Growth is Behind the Industry Average

When we buy a house one of our goals is to build equity for the future. We do this in two ways. The first is by paying down the principal of the mortgage so we will eventually own our home outright and the 2nd is hoping that the value of the home will increase enough while we own it so that we can either trade up to a bigger and better house or use our equity for retirement or other lifestyle choices. Buyers of businesses are no different. Yes, they are buying the future cash flow of a business, but they also want to be able to sell it for more than what they paid. They can accomplish this by increasing profits margins as we already discussed but they can also accomplish this by increasing sales. As an owner you don't have a lot of control of the growth of your industry, but you do have a lot of control on the growth rate of your business. If it is discovered that your company's growth rate is behind the industry average it could be a sign that you are losing market share which could take a lot of investment time and money for a new owner to get the market share back. A growing business also gives the new buyer comfort in knowing that their investment is likely to grow. Just a further note about growth. Besides benchmarking your company's growth against industry average, a buyer will also assess if your industry is growing or in decline. A declining industry often takes down companies with it and may prove to be a bad investment. Here is a simple case in point, Blockbuster once dominated the brick and mortar home video industry but as it disappeared so did Blockbuster with the exception of one lone location in Alaska (as of the writing of this book).

3. You & Your Staff are Constantly Fighting Fires

Do any of these sound familiar? You constantly get customer complaints for poor service or shipping errors, missed deadlines, running out of stock of popular items, invoicing errors or paper work not getting done. If you answered "yes" to any of these, you are either lacking systems or have poorly developed systems in one or more areas of your business. There should be documented systems for every process in your business and your staff should be properly trained to follow your system. This is the only way to ensure that details don't fall through the cracks creating a crisis every ten minutes. If you don't have comprehensive systems already installed in your business a new buyer will have to invest time and money to do so and will want a steep discount as compensation.

4. You Can't Take a Day Off or a Vacation for Fear that the "Wheels will Fall Off"

Let me be blunt. Telling people that you haven't had a day off for weeks or have not taken a vacation in years is not a badge of honour. It does not mean that you are superman with great abilities. It means that you are running an ineffective business. Everybody waits for your approval to do just about anything and if you're not available nothing happens. Tell me, how many buyers want to own a business where they will have to work every day without a day off or not be able to take a vacation for years? Most will run for the hills. If this describes your situation it is a sign that your business lacks organizational structure and that you have failed to have properly trained and developed your staff to handle many of the tasks that you currently do yourself. This can have a bigger effect on the value of your business than you think and is a clear sign that you are running a fixer upper.

5. You are the Face of the Business to Your Clients or Suppliers

Here is a hint to know if this applies to you. Your customers and suppliers call you directly on a regular basis to conduct routine business transactions instead of calling your team. They like the personal touch you give and would likely not do business with your business if you were not there. In other words, the relationships are with you and not the business. This will have a significant effect on the value of your business because there is a high risk to the buyer that the business could lose many customers if they can't deal with you. You may not be able to avoid this if you have a micro business (less than five employees) but if you have more than five employees it might be time to build some structure in your business so you can start divesting yourself of daily interaction with clients and suppliers. It might be necessary for you to be involved in negotiating contracts, but the ongoing transactions should flow through your team.

Relationships with suppliers should not be overlooked, especially if they are the only source for key components of your products. I know of a distributor that had exclusive rights to its key product. The business was able to secure the rights based on the owners long standing relationship with the supplier. When the owner sold his business, the supplier pulled the key product from the distributorship only weeks after the original owner left the business. One half of the business value disappeared for the new owner overnight with the loss of the key product and there was nothing the new owner could do. The bottom line is to make your business the brand and not yourself.

6.   You Would be Lost Without That One Key Employee

I know of an IT services company that had grown very quickly, won awards for customer service and was very well known in the community. The issue was that the owner was not a computer tech by trade and employed some high-quality techs to serve customers. In most cases this would not be a problem but there was one tech who was the "tech brain" of the company and was the primary service provider to the company's largest customer who represented almost half of its business. One day this key technician realized that his boss needed him more than he needed his boss, so he quit, started his own IT services business and took the key client with him. Without the key tech or the key client, the business started to unravel and was out of business within twenty-four months.

You might be a little confused because I just said that that customers should not deal directly with the owner if possible. There are two dynamics to deal with here. First, don't let an employee be the only one to have access to the "secret sauce" of your company. Try to establish a team approach to dealing with clients, especially the key ones. This way if one person does leave, the client still feels they have a relationship with your business through the other team members. Although you don't want to get involved in daily transactions it is prudent for the key client to at least know who you are so you can reach out to them if there is a change. It is imperative that you build succession into each job so you have someone on the team who can take over the lead position. If your key employee is so unique and key to the business that it isn't possible to build succession into the position, then consider "soft handcuffs". These are strategies that makes it very difficult for the key person to leave. A couple common methods include giving or selling the key person an equity position in the business, so they become a minority partner or at the very least have them sign a Non-Disclosure Agreement (NDA) that legally prevents them from soliciting your customers or divulging your company's secrets. These agreements need to be carefully worded to be enforceable so consult your legal advisor before proceeding.

7.   You Keep Losing Talented People

No one expects employment with a company for life anymore, so employee turnover is acceptable. But what is acceptable? Every industry has its own benchmarks for acceptable turnover, so the key is to benchmark your company's turnover against the industry average. If your turnover is less than the average, then great. If it is on par with the average it might be OK but there is probably room for improvement. If your turnover is higher than the industry average, it is very likely that there is a lot of room for improvement. So, what causes higher than average turnover? Here is a hint. Studies have shown that most people don't quit their job, they leave their boss. Poor leadership and management are a key reason for employee turnover. If your turnover is higher than average, then either you or your management team is causing this to happen. Refer to the chapters on leadership earlier in this book for some insight into how you or your team can be more effective leaders and managers.

8.   You Are the Intellectual Property for the Business. (the one with all the knowledge)

This is like that key employee who has the secret sauce to the business inside his head except <u>you</u> are the key employee. You are the only one who has intimate knowledge of your products, all systems are in your head and everyone comes to you for answers. Chances are that you're very busy every day, but you don't feel like you accomplish anything. If this describes you it is a strong indication that your business doesn't have adequate, if any, documented systems for your team to follow. I always use the "hit by a bus" rule when working with my clients. It goes like this, ask yourself what would happen to your business if you got hit by a bus? The key is to get the information out of your head and onto paper so you can teach and develop your team to do what you do. If you don't do this your business and everything you have worked for could fall apart if you are unable to work for any reason.

It's All About the Risk to the Buyer

You have probably noticed as you read this chapter that the common theme is risk. The higher the risk that future cash flow of the business will not be sustained the less a buyer will be willing to pay for the business. All the above signs of a fixer upper pose a risk to a buyer of a business. If any of these signs apply to your business, then come up with a plan to minimize those risks to the buyer and they will be willing to pay more for your business. The good news is that as you address the risks to the buyer you will also find your business will run much more smoothly, make more money today, giving you the work/life balance, you seek while building value for the future.

Chapter 12

Understanding Financial Statements

Life is about balance

I was meeting with a business owner when we agreed to review his most current financial statements so we could have a better understanding of the financial state of his business and make some key decisions. He reached into the drawer of his desk and pulled out a neat file containing his financial statements. As he flipped through the papers, he removed a couple pages, put them to the side and said, "I don't know why my accountant keeps giving me this, I never look at it". The removed pages were the balance sheet. He then pulled out the Profit & Loss Statement (P&L) took a quick look at it and said," I look at the sales and net profit to see if I am making money, but I don't understand what the rest is about". Does this sound familiar to you? I hear it all the time from business owners in every industry and all business sizes.

The purpose of this chapter is not to turn you into an accountant but to be sure that you are comfortable reading financial statements so you can understand the story between the lines. Knowing your financial story will help you to better understand the state of your business allowing you to make more informed decisions to improve profitability, cash flow and overall performance. The reason everyone calls them financial statements instead of one financial statement is because they include three separate statements. They include: Profit & Loss (P&L), Balance Sheet and Statement of Cash Flows. There are others, but these are the major three.

Profit & Loss Statements (P&L)

Fig 12.1

	Current Period	Prior Period
Gross Revenue	2,380,456	1,960,546
Cost of Sales (exclude any depreciation)	1,547,296	1,275,965
Gross Profit	833,160	684,581
General and Administrative Expenses		
Sales & Marketing	105,868	108,548
Insurance	15,197	13,844
Office & Admin Salaries	266,789	258,622
Rent	94,852	92,599
Utilities	19,122	18,546
Total Expenses	501,828	492,159
Earnings before Income Tax, Interest, Depreciation and Amortization (EBITDA)	331,332	192,422
Income Tax	0	0
Interest	1,421	109
Depreciation	2,868	3,052
Amortization	0	0
Net Income	327,043	189,261
Number of Full Time Employees	12	11

The purpose of a P&L is to show how a business performed over a defined amount of time. Most P&Ls, whether produced by your accountant or internally from your bookkeeping software will state the time period the statement represents with a start date and end date. For example, if the stated financial period is a calendar year it will say, "January 1, 20_ _ to December 31, 20 _ _.

There are five key sections in a Profit & Loss Statement as shown if *Fig 12.1* that include: *Income/Sales, Cost of Goods Sold (COGS),*

Gross Profit, Operating/Fixed Expenses and *Net Profit*. I often find that business owners are confused about the difference between Gross Profit and Net Profit or between Cost of Goods Sold and Operating/ Fixed Expenses so let's clarify these differences right now.

Income/Sales
This is the top line that appears on your P&L Statement. Depending on who is creating the statement this line could be labeled as Income, Sales, Revenue or any other way that the creator wants to identify it. In some cases, it will show Revenue, then subtracts Discounts or Returns to show Net Revenue. At the end of the day it represents the sales your business generated in the stated time period.

Cost of Goods Sold (COGS)
This part of the P&L tends to cause the most confusion amongst business owners, bookkeepers and at times, even accountants. I often see expenses that should be part of COGS stuffed in the General Operating Expenses section of the P&L. Let's stop the confusion once and for all and agree on the following definition of COGS.

> *A Cost of Goods Sold includes <u>all direct expenses</u> incurred to produce a product or to perform a service. This includes but is not limited to production labour, parts, packaging, labels, travel costs to serve the customer, operating costs of service vehicles etc.*

A more detailed explanation of what items are included in COGS can be found in *Chapter 8, Increasing Gross Profits*. If the COGS section of the P&L you receive from your accountant or bookkeeper doesn't seem to reflect the description in this book it is suggested that you ask your accountant about it. They might have a perfectly logical explanation about why certain items in COGS are missing but it is equally possible that it has been overlooked. Based on the level of service you have with your accountant it is possible they may see their role to simply take the information you gave and produce the statement. Any other type of advice or direction would be considered consulting and would cost extra. If your discussion with your accountant reveals that certain items are indeed missing from COGS, they can make the necessary adjustments to the P&L and advise your bookkeeper on how to adjust the books, so the information is produced in the correct format.

Gross Profit
Gross Profit is what is left over after you sold your product or performed your service and incurred the expenses included in your COGS. This is a matter of a simple calculation

Gross Profit = Revenue – COGS.

Operating Expenses
This category of expenses tends to confuse some people because it can be called different names depending on who you are talking to. Besides being called Operating Expenses, other popular names include Fixed Costs, Overhead and Indirect Expenses. Each name gives a different connotation of which expenses it includes but it is all the same. Here is a layman's definition of Operating Expenses:

> *Operating Expenses, also known as Fixed Expenses or Overhead are expenses that are not directly incurred when producing a product or delivering a service but are still incurred whether a product was produced, or a service delivered.*

Some examples of Operating Expenses include rent, office and management salaries, insurance, property taxes, office supplies and utilities

Net Profit/Loss
Very little explanation needed here. You're either making it or you not. This is a simple math equation:

Net Profit (Loss) = Revenue – (COGS + Operating Expenses)

The Balance Sheet

Fig 12.2

Your Company				Dec-31				
	Current	**Prior**				**Current**	**Prior**
	Period	**Period**				**Period**	**Period**
ASSETS				**LIABILITIES**			
Current Assets				**Current Liabilities**			
Cash and Equivalents	88,546	68,584		Accounts Payable	91,156	97,844
Accounts Receivable	133,844	171,531		Accrued Expenses	14,874	15,963
Inventory	389,466	403,572		Short Term Notes Payable	45,000	50,000
Prepaid Expenses	11,212	0		Current Portion of LT Debt	7,000	9,000
Total Current Assets	**623,068**	**643,687**		**Total Current Liabilities**	**158,030**	**172,807**
Fixed Assets				**Long Term Liabilities**			
Land	41,521	41,521		Notes Payable to Lenders	48,000	55,000
Buildings	246,526	246,526		Loans from Stockholders	100,000	110,000
Machinery & Equipment	170,698	170,698				
Furniture and Fixtures	28,989	27,588		**Total Long Term Liabilities**	**148,000**	**165,000**
Vehicles	117,895	117,895				
Office Equipment	27,853	26,562				
Total Fixed Assets	633,482	630,790				
Less: Accum Dep	488,633	423,521		**Total Liabilities**	**306,030**	**337,807**
Net Fixed Assets	144,849	207,269				
				EQUITY			
				Stock	61,175	61,175
				Retained Earnings	400,712	451,974
				Total Equity	**461,887**	**513,149**
Total Assets	**767,917**	**850,956**		**Total Liabilities & Equity**	**767,917**	**850,956**

If you have ever presented your financial statements to a banker during the process of securing financing, you may have noticed them doing something weird. Unlike the confused business owner who put the balance sheet to the side when looking at his financial statements the banker will immediately look at your balance sheet and perform some quick calculations as you start to sweat. He will then react with either a frown or smile before proceeding with the conversation. Now you are wondering, "What the heck is so special about that mysterious balance sheet"? It is important because it clearly shows if your business can pay its bills, how much debt you have and how much "skin you have in the game", all of which are not only very important to a banker but should be even more important to you.

Unlike a Profit and Loss Statement which shows the business performance over a period of time, the Balance Sheet is a picture of the financial state of a business on a certain day. When looking at your company's balance sheet you will notice there no date range given but instead, it does show a specific date. For example, if the Balance Sheet is based on the financial state of the business on December 31 of a specific year it will say, "As of December,31, 20_ _.

As shown in *Fig 12.2*, a Balance Sheet is split into three sections, each with its own sub categories. The major sections are: *Assets, Liabilities and Equity*. Let's examine each section, sub categories and their importance.

Assets
Assets are items that the company owns and is split into two categories called *Current Assets* and *Fixed Assets*. Current Assets are items that can change on a daily basis as the business completes transactions. This includes cash on hand, accounts receivable and inventory. Fixed Assets are items that usually don't change in the short term with only the occasional change made when the business makes a major move such as buying or selling capital items. Examples of Fix Assets include owned land and buildings, machinery, vehicles and even leasehold improvements made to a rented property.

Liabilities
Just like Assets, there are two categories of Liabilities: *Current Liabilities and Long Terms Liabilities*. Current Liabilities are the debts the business needs to pay in the short term, usually within a year and includes items such as Accounts Payable, taxes, wages and salaries incurred but not yet paid and loan payments. Long Term liabilities are debts that need to be paid in the long term, usually past one year and includes items such as mortgage balances, long term loans for capital equipment and loans made by shareholders to the company ie. Shareholder Loans.

Shareholder's Equity

Let's use your own personal net worth as an example. If you were to add up all your assets such as your home, car, furniture and investments and subtracted all the money you owed such as mortgages, loans and credit cards the difference would be your net worth. For example, if your if your assets were worth $1M and your total liabilities including mortgages, loans and credit cards were $700K your net worth would be $300K. Shareholders Equity is very similar to your personal net worth but in the case of your business it the amount of equity that you have tied up in your business. In other words, it is what is left over when you deduct all the business's liabilities from its assets.

When looking at the Shareholders Equity Section of the balance sheet you will notice a few items under the Shareholders Equity section: Share Value, Retained Earnings. Share Value is the actual amount the shares were sold for. For example, if you bought 100 shares at $1.00 each the Share Value would be $100. This number usually stays constant unless new shares were sold.

Retained Earnings are all the profits that have accumulated since inception of the business but have not yet been paid to the shareholders. Business owners often choose to keep profits in the business for several reasons such as preserving cash to invest in the future growth of the company, insufficient available cash to facilitate the payout (see the Chapter 10, Cash is King) or as part of a tax deferral strategy recommended by the accountant or financial planner. Your accountant might also recommend paying yourself a combination of Salary, bonus and dividends to minimize your tax exposure based on local tax laws.

Total Shareholder Equity is the sum of Share Value and all past profits not yet withdrawn ie. Retained Earnings. You will notice in *Figure 12.2*, that the total amount of Assets exactly matches the amount of Liabilities and Shareholder Equity. This is the reason this statement is called a balance sheet. If the two sides don't balance it is a clear indication that some numbers shown are not correct and the statement isn't accurate. Don't automatically assume that a balanced statement is accurate. There could still be errors even if the statement is balanced. For example, some items on the same side of the balance sheet could be miss assigned such as current liabilities being stated as long-term liabilities or vice versa. This wouldn't affect the total balance on the Total Liabilities & Equity side, but it would cause some important ratio calculations to be inaccurate. This will be explained in more detail in the 8 *Key Financial Numbers You Must Know* section below.

9 Key Financial Numbers You Must Know

When we receive financial statements from our accountant or bookkeeper it is natural to first look at the total revenue and net profit of the P&L. Let's be honest, we get an adrenaline rush as we anticipate seeing what the numbers will look like. I must admit I do the same thing whenever I look at a client's financial statement for the first time. Once the adrenaline rush has passed there are a few quick calculations you need to do that will give you a deeper insight into how your business is doing. Unlike KPIs that are ratios providing detailed insight into operations, the 8 key numbers are financial calculations that provide a bird's eye view of how your business is doing and will provide you with the information needed to determine which areas of the business need more attention.

Four of the key numbers are calculated directly from the P&L, two are calculated directly from the Balance Sheet and three numbers require both statements. The key numbers are listed below based on the required financial statement.

Profit & Loss Statement
The three key numbers calculated from the P&L are: *Gross Profit Margin, Net Profit Margin, Percent of Fixed Costs to Sales* and the *Break Even Point.* If Gross Profit Margin and Net Profit Margin sound familiar it is because we covered them in Chapter 5, The Magic Profit

Formula. For convenience sake I have listed them again below followed by Percent of Fixed Cost to Sales.

Gross Margin

Gross Margin is *Gross Profit* stated as a percentage of sales. Gross Profit is calculated by subtracting the Cost of Goods Sold from Sales.

Let's apply this formula to the example in *Figure 12.1*. In this case the gross profit in the current period is $833,160 with sales of $2,380,456. If we divide the gross profit by sales as shown in the formula below the gross margin is 35%. Apply this formula to your P&L to determine your gross margin. How does it look? How does it compare to your industry? If you are not happy, its time to take some action.

$$\frac{\$833,160\ (Gross\ Profit)}{\$2,380,456\ (Revenue)} \times 100 = 35\%\ (Gross\ Margin)$$

Fixed Costs to Sales

Knowing the percentage of fixed costs to sales is important because it serves as a barometer to determine if your fixed costs are in line with sales. For example, if your sales are decreasing the percentage of fixed costs to sales will increase indicating that you might have to make some cuts. On the other hand, if sales are increasing the percentage should drop or at least remain the same. If you find the fixed cost percentage increasing while sales are increasing, you could be adding more fixed costs than needed.

In the current period in the sample P&L we can see that when we divide the total fixed costs of $501,828 by sales of $2,380,456 the percentage of fixed costs to sales is 21%. If we do the same calculation for the previous period, the percentage of fixed costs to sales is 25% ($492,159/1,960,546). By comparing the percentage of fixed costs to sales we can see that the percentage decrease from the prior year to the current year. This is good news because it shows that fixed costs are increasing slower than sales growth which shows that the company is controlling fixed costs and is improving net profits.

Net Profit Margin

Net Profit is that number we all look forward to seeing. This is your return for risking an investment in your business and after all that hard work. It is calculated by subtracting all those Cost of Goods Sold and Fixed Expenses from Revenue. Net Profit Margin as shown in the formula below is the percentage of net profit divided by sales.

$$\frac{Net\ Profit}{Sales} \times 100 = Net\ Profit\ Margin$$

When we apply this formula to current period in the sample P&L the Net Profit Margin is 13.7%.

$$\frac{\$327{,}043\ (Net\ Profit)}{\$2{,}380{,}456\ (Sales)} \times 100 = 13.7\%$$

When we plug the numbers from the prior period into this formula the Net Profit Margin is 9.6%. It is easy to see that net profit margins are growing. Are your net profits margins growing? If not, you have significant leaks in the bucket to fix.

Break Even Point

The *Break Even Point (BEP)* is a very key number because it tells you how much you need to sell to cover all your costs. If your business is not at least breaking even it means that you are going deeper and deeper into a hole. It means you will have to either go further into debt or invest more money into the business just keep operating. Although your ultimate goal is to make a profit, your first goal is to be sure you are at least breaking even. The formula for calculating your BEP is straight forward and is found below.

$$\frac{Fixed\ Cost}{Gross\ Margin} = Break\ Even\ Point$$

Let's apply this to our example where the Fixed Costs were $501,828 and the Gross Margin was 35%.

$$\frac{\$501,828}{.35} = \$1,433,794$$

Remember that all the direct costs incurred to produce your product or complete your service are covered in COGS which was 65% of the sale leaving the business 35% of the sale (Gross Profit) to pay its fixed costs. If 35% of every sale goes to paying fixed costs this means the business needs to sell $1,433,794 in product or services just to cover all its costs. You might have heard some propeller heads referring to "contribution to overhead". Until you have generated enough gross profit to cover your fixed costs, gross profits are just contributing to overhead. Once you have reached the BEP, your gross margins now become net profit.

The reason it is so important to plug the profit holes in your business is because your BEP decreases for every percentage point that the gross margin is increased. Let's take a quick look at the BEP if the gross margin was increased to 40%

$$\frac{\$501,828}{.40} = \$1,254,570$$

The BEP is reduced by almost $180,000 ($1,433,794-$1,254,570) just by increasing gross margins from 35% to 40%. This means that you are now breaking-even much faster and all the gross margins you make after selling $1,254,570 becomes Net Profit! Are you getting excited?

Balance Sheet
There are two very important numbers to know that come directly from the balance sheet. They are the *Current Ratio* and the *Debt to Equity Ratio*.

Current Ratio

The Current Ratio provides quick feedback on your business's ability to pay its bills. As covered in Chapter 10, *Cash is King*, your business can be shut down quickly if your suppliers cut you off or if your employees walk out. The formula is simple, just divide your Current Assets by Current Liabilities. Let's apply this calculation using the numbers from *Figure 19.*

$$\frac{\$623,068\ (Current\ Assets)}{\$158,030\ (Current\ Liabilities)} = 3.9$$

As we can see above, the Current Ratio is 3.9. This means that there is 3.9X more cash, receivables and inventory available than bills to be paid. If the ratio was less than 1, it would mean the business will not be able to pay all its bills and is in big trouble. What if the number is 1? It means that you are living hand to mouth and are likely already in a cash flow crunch. So, what is a healthy number? It depends on who you are talking to but a number between 1.5X to 2X or better is considered acceptable. If the number is very high it might indicate that you have the extra cash available to either reinvest in the business or to withdraw for your own use. Check with your accountant to confirm if your current ratio number is good for your business.

Debt to Equity Ratio

Debt/Equity Ratio indicates the relationship between the level of debt your business is carrying compared to amount of equity in the business. It confirms whether your business operations are funded by investment or through debt. It also provides feedback on the ownership's ability to cover the debt and the level of risk to the bank if there was a decrease in business. This ratio is calculated by dividing Total Liabilities by Shareholder's Equity. Using the sample balance sheet, the calculation would look as follows:

$$\frac{\$306,030\ (Total\ Liabilities)}{\$461,887\ (Total\ Equity)} = .66$$

A D/E Ratio of .66 means that there is about 50% more equity than debt. To many this would be a very favorable number because it means there is much more equity than debt and the business would have no problem covering its debt if there was a down turn. This does not necessarily mean that a D/E ratio of over 1.0 is bad. Just as many people have mortgages on their home that are several times larger than the equity in the home, it is also acceptable for businesses to have more debt than equity. This is called *leveraging*. The question comes down to what an acceptable D/E ratio is. This varies by industry with the acceptable amount affected by several factors such as the amount of capital equipment required to operate the business. If a million-dollar machine is required to produce a product, a company might have to use debt (a loan) to buy it which would increase the ratio. Do some research or talk with your accountant to determine the acceptable D/E ratio for your business.

Profit & Loss/Balance Sheet
For the following key calculations, you will need the Profit & Loss Statement and the Balance Sheet side by side.

<u>Return on Equity</u>
Return on Equity (ROE)is the relationship between the profits your business generates and the amount of resources you have invested in the business. When we own a business our first goal is to be able to pay ourselves market rate for the job we have in our business. For example, if you act as the general manager of your business you want to be able to pay yourself the same salary that a general manager running a company of your size in your industry would be paid. With this achieved, the next step is to get a return on investment for all the financial and emotional risk you have taken.

Let's use the Current Period of the financial statements in *Figures 12.1 and 12.2* to demonstrate how to calculate ROE.

$$\frac{\$327{,}043 \text{ (Net Income from P\&L)}}{\$461{,}887 \text{ (Equity from Balance Sheet)}} \times 100 = 71\% \text{ (ROE)}$$

If we apply the same formula to the Prior Period, the ROE would be 37% (($189,261/$513,149) X 100)). Are these ROEs acceptable? The answer is, it depends. Here is an example, if I told you my business made a $1M profit would you be impressed? It sure sounds like a lot of money. Consider this, if I had $20M invested in the business a profit of $1M is a 5% ROE. Would you be happy with this knowing that you could possibly invest the same $20M in another investment vehicle and earn 15% to 20% ROE?

It is important to remember that the equity you have in your business is an investment. The above examples show a ROE of 71% and 37%. We need to compare this with the returns being offered in the market place now? Chances are you would be hard pressed in most economic times to achieve this level of return assuming the business is not a high-risk investment. What is the ROE of your business? Is it providing a higher return than if you invested your equity outside your business? If so, is the difference large enough to justify the risk you take by having all the eggs in your own basket? Its OK if you are not happy with your ROE because that is what this book is all about. We are here to help you increase profits so you can improve your ROE.

Accounts Receivable Turns

Knowing your *Accounts Receivable Turns* is important because it indicates if you have too much of your sales going unpaid which can provide some answers if you are struggling with cash flow.

To calculate A/R turns you first need to know the average Accounts Receivable for the year. This is calculated as follows:

$$\frac{Beginning\ A/R\ Balance + Ending\ A/R\ Balance}{2} = Average\ Accounts\ Receivable$$

Now with your average A/R in hand you are now ready to calculate you're A/R turns with this simple formula.

$$\frac{Net\ Annual\ Credit\ Sales}{Average\ A/R}$$

Using the Current Period in Figures 12.1 and 12.2 let's assume that 50% of sales on made on Net 30 and the other 50% is cash sales. the A/R Turns would be calculated as follows:

The average A/R is:

$$\underline{\$171,531 \text{ (Beginning A/R)} + \$133,844 \text{ (Ending A/R)}} = \$152,687.50$$
$$2$$

$$\underline{\$1,190,228 \text{ (Credit Sales)}} = 7.80$$
$$\$152,687.50 \text{ (Average A/R)}$$

Let's put A/R turns into perspective before commenting on what an A/R turn of 7.80 means. If we consider one turn to be an average 30 period from when an invoice is created, then there are 12 turns per year. If a company has 12.0 A/R turns it means that very close to 100% of sales sold on credit are being collected in the 30-day cycle. If the turns are 2.0, money is being collected in about 6 months; 4.0 turns are 3 month and 6.0 turns are 2 months.

In the above example, 7.80 turns mean that it is taking 1.54 cycles (about 1.5 months) to be paid. To calculate the number of cycles just divide the number of turns into the number 12 i.e. (12/Turns). In this case 12 divided by 7.80 is 1.54. Because the average cycle is 30 days, 1.54 cycles is about 6 weeks. If this business is expected to pay its vendor's invoices in 30 days, it needs a plan to have enough cash to operate during the two-week gap. Remember the "Cash Gap" in Chapter 10. This is one of the first calculations I do when a business owner complains about cash flow. Assuming the company has Net 30 terms any turnover less than 12 usually means that the company needs to do a better job collecting its money or at least have a plan to cover the "the gap".

Inventory Turns
Knowing your *Inventory Turns* is important because it indicates if you are carrying too much inventory which could be causing a cash flow crunch.

The formula for calculating Inventory Turns is:

$$\frac{Cost\ of\ Goods\ Sold}{Ending\ Inventory}$$

If we apply this formula to the Current Period of the financial statement example the calculation will look like this:

$$\frac{\$1,547,296\ (Cost\ of\ Goods\ Sold)}{\$389,466\ (Ending\ Inventory)} = 3.97$$

Just like A/R turns, any turn rate less than 12 means that you are sitting on inventory past the 30-day cycle. In this example the company's inventory turns are 3.97 or just under 4.0 which means the business is carrying about 3 months of inventory at any given time. Every industry has a generally acceptable level of inventory turns so you will need to decide if carrying inventory past 30 days is necessary for your business. Keep in mind that if you need to carry inventory past one cycle you will need a plan to cover "the gap" until you sell it and get paid.

If you are seeing the importance of tracking these numbers, I suggest creating a simple one-page analysis form like the one shown in *Fig 12.3*, that you or someone you can delegate it to, can fill out every month.

Fig 12.3

Financial Analysis Summary

P&L	
Sales _____ A	
Credit Sales _____ A1	
COGS _____ B	
Gross Profit _____ C	
Fixed Costs _____ D	
Net Profit _____ E	

Balance Sheet	
Current Assets _____ F	
Inventory (Current Period) _____ G	
Inventory (Previous Period) _____ H	
A/R (Current Period) _____ I	
A/R (Previous Period) _____ J	
Current Liabilities _____ K	
Total Liabilities _____ L	
Total Equity _____ M	

Calculations

1. Gross Margin: (C/A) X 100 = _____ % N
2. Net Margin: (E/A) X 100 = _____ %
3. Fixed Cost to Sales: (D/A) X 100 _____ %
4. Break Even Point: (D/N) _____ $
5. Current Ratio: (F/K) _____
6. D/E Ratio: (L/M) _____
7. Return on Equity: (E/M) _____%
8. Average A/R: (I + J)/2 _____ O
9. A/R Turns: (A1/O) _____
10. Average Inventory: (G + H)/2 _____P
11. Inventory Turns: (P/B) _____

Chapter 13

Get off The Mouse Wheel

Round...round we go

Many business owners I speak with describe how running their business feels like they are running on a mouse wheel. They keep their nose to a grind stone, working very long, hard hours. They are constantly fighting fires as they deal with everything from sales & marketing, customer service, accounting, bank deposits, government regulations, people problems and even getting on the tools during times of crisis.

Finally, the day is over, they are exhausted and after looking back on the day, the month or even the year(s), they wonder if they are ever going to get ahead. Does this sound familiar? If your answer is yes, you are not alone. Many (probably most) business owners deal with this all the time. I have good news, there is a better way and hope is on the horizon.

I worked with the owner of a manufacturing company that was working sixty to seventy hours per week. He was stressed out and although the business was very profitable, he had begun to resent it. The business had experienced phenomenal growth with annual sales increasing from $1M to over $7M in about 8 years. It went from employing ten employees to over thirty in that time. In the early days the owner would help where ever he was needed. He would ship and receive product, do the bank deposits and even help to stuff invoices into envelopes. Guess what? He was doing the exact same tasks while running a $7M per year company. He did a fantastic job growing sales but failed to build a sustainable structure into his business.

In his book "The E Myth Revisited", Michael E. Gerber talks about the three personalities of the business owner: *The Entrepreneur, The Manager* and *The Technician*.

The Entrepreneur is that crazy person in you that said, "I'm going to fire my boss and start my own business" or "I'm going to buy that business". The Entrepreneur is the dreamer, the visionary, the one who has a goal and result in mind. The entrepreneur is the one who made the decision to put everything on the line, to take the financial and emotional risk to build a better future and leave a legacy.

The Manager in you oversees the day to day activities of the business to ensure that the mouse wheel is progressing in the direction set by the entrepreneur. The manager is the analytical one, the one who sees the obstacles, creates the action plans and measures performance, making any adjustments as necessary.

When in Technician mode, you are the person who has specialized technical knowledge and works "in the business". You are on the tools, producing the product and even shipping it yourself. In the beginning you probably were in technician mode most of the time and without you the business would stop running. If you currently find yourself frustrated and overwhelmed by your business, it is very likely that you are still running your business the same way you did when you started out. As your business grew you kept doing the same tasks you always did. It is comfortable and you know how to do those tasks very well. You still spend a lot of your time in technician model despite having employees around you. Does any of this sound familiar?

Each personality in you represents a different value to your business. The Technician is a task-oriented role where the value of the position is based on the amount someone would be paid to do the same job. For example, if the business is a plumbing company the value of the Technician is what a plumber is typically paid or in the case of a manufacturer the value of the technician would be the wage paid to production staff.

Depending on the industry, the general rule of thumb for determining the value of the Manager's tasks is to double the value of the Technician value. The Entrepreneurs value is often double or more than the value of the Manager.

Why is this? The value of a task is measured by the level of impact and long-term effect it can have on the success of the business. The Technician's tasks will usually have a short-term effect on the business whereas the Entrepreneur's tasks usually involve key decisions that can have a significant long-term impact on the business.

In the case of the manufacturer in my example, I explained the concept of the three personalities of the business owner to him and he immediately realized that he was spending over 80% of his time in technician mode. He was ready and more than motivated to make the necessary changes in his business so he could spend 80% of his time in management and entrepreneur modes but didn't know where and how to start. I explained the seven-step business transformation process and we got started. Here is what we did and how we did it.

Fig 13.1

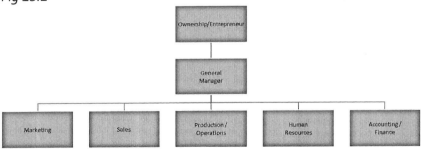

I showed him a diagram like the one in *Figure 13.1* and explained that every business has the same basic structure. Every business has an owner(s), general manager and departments that include marketing, sales, operations, customer service and finance & administration. In a very small business, the owner may fill all these roles but as the business grows the he must remove himself from these roles and start to delegate the associated tasks to others. In our manufacturers case, besides being the owner and general manager, he was also the marketing department, sales department and spent countless hours helping in all the other departments. No wonder he was working longs hours and getting stressed out.

It wasn't realistic for the owner to immediately remove himself from all the roles, so we set some priorities. I asked him what tasks he enjoyed doing the most as well as which offered the highest value to the success of his company. It was clear, evidenced by the growth of sales that one of his biggest strengths and passions was sales and marketing. His least favorite tasks involved finance, administration and the hands-on aspect of operations but they all needed his help. The first step was to have the owner identify all the roles in his company and list all the tasks of each job. We started with the tasks he did every day. As we listed all his tasks it became apparent that he was spending more time working on tasks belonging to other roles than those of a general manager. With his very long list of tasks completed I asked him to assign a value to each task by asking himself this simple question. How much would he pay someone to do each task if he didn't do it himself. We found that about forty percent of the tasks were worth less than one half of what a general manager in his industry was being paid. In other words, he was spending forty percent of his time on tasks worth less than half of his paygrade.

Before we could start assigning the lower valued tasks to others, we needed to determine where all the roles in the company fit on the organization chart. With this lengthy exercise completed, we assigned the lower valued tasks to the appropriate positions. I bet you think this was the end and everyone lived happily ever after. The fact is that this was only the beginning. Everything we did up to now was just theory. It was now time for the rubber to hit the road. We now had to go through the long and painstaking exercise of the owner letting go of these tasks and start the delegation process.

Delegating tasks can go very badly if not properly done. It might be straight forward to assign the task of stuffing envelopes to someone but what about more complicated tasks. For instance, if an owner determines he needs to delegate inventory tracking, how does he do it? Does he walk over to someone in operations and says," Here are the inventory tracking forms and spreadsheets, I would like you to look after these from now on", then walks away thinking, great I just delegated? How do you think this will go? The person who is now responsible for tracking inventory may be very smart but without training and direction they could end up doing the job very differently than how the owner wanted it done or may have no idea what they are doing in the first place, causing turmoil. When the owner realizes the inventory control system is all messed up, he becomes frustrated and says that this delegation is "for the birds" and takes it all back returning to doing it himself.

To prevent this from happening to the manufacturer, we listed each task that was going to be delegated and determined what skills and knowledge were required to perform the task competently. We then assessed the skill set and knowledge level of the individual who was going to be assigned the task to see if any training was needed. With the plan and assessment completed, we determined the type of training or briefing needed and started meeting with the appropriate individuals to delegate the tasks.

Ok, so with the individuals now properly trained I bet you think the delegation process is over and everyone will now live happily ever after. Not quite yet. Just because you delegated a task it doesn't mean that you don't track performance and continually follow up. In the case of tracking inventory, you might want the individual to report back to you after they complete each step to ensure they understand the task, so you can correct them if they did misunderstand how to do it, thus preventing them from messing up the whole system. It is OK to have them report back less and less as they demonstrate their understanding and competence to perform the task. If you are assigning a task to someone who already has the experience and knowledge to perform it, you could choose to meet only occasionally to help with any challenges or to just review the result. Either way, it is still your job to ensure these tasks are being done correctly so having a reporting system that allows you to quickly review the result is important. For example, with inventory control you could ask for a monthly inventory report and review it to see if there are any inconsistencies. People "respect what you inspect" so if your staff knows you are reviewing their results, they are more likely to take the necessary care and attention to be sure it is done correctly.

By following this process our manufacturing friend was able to successfully delegate the lower value tasks with only a few minor hiccups along the way. The result was he was able to reduce his work load by forty percent, reduce his workweek from over sixty hours to about forty-five hours and most importantly, his stress was dramatically reduced. The manufacturer continues to look after sales and marketing because he enjoys it and he can fit it into his day. As his business continues to grow it will become challenging for him to continue looking after sales and marketing and he will have to eventually create a full-time sales position so he can solely focus on his general manager duties.

You are probably thinking that this is a lot of work. Perhaps it is easier to just keep doing what you are currently doing. Think of the delegation process as an investment of time. It will probably take the initial delegation of the task longer than doing the task yourself but once you make the investment of time, you will get back that time hundreds and even thousands of times over. For example, let's assume you were spending two hours per week on inventory control and it would take you four hours to train the new person. There would be an investment of an additional two hours for training, but you would now save the original two hours per week every week resulting in 104 hours saved per year, every year. You can now use your new-found time to focus on performing more valuable tasks that will add value to your business or choose to use it to do something really crazy like having dinner with your family.

Keep in mind that this whole process didn't happen in a few days. It took about three months to get the whole delegation plan in place and about another three months to execute the delegation plan and get everyone up to speed on their new tasks. Try applying the steps we took to your business. How can you start removing yourself from technician mode and focusing on those tasks worthy of your paygrade? I have provided a summary of the steps below for your convenience.

1. Create an organization chart of your business
2. Create a Job Description for all roles in the company (including yours)
3. List every task that you do (even stuffing envelopes)
4. Analyse every task you do to determine the value of the task
5. Establish a plan of to delegate your low value tasks and add them to the job description of the position you are delegating to
6. Start delegating
7. Monitor and adjust

Assemble an Effective & Productive Leadership Team

Most of us like to surround ourselves with likeminded people and tend to hire those who remind us of ourselves. If we are outgoing, we like to surround ourselves with high energy people. If we are introverted, we prefer people who are also lower energy but more thoughtful. We do this because its comfortable and if people think like us, they will agree with us. The danger of surrounding yourself with those who always agree with you or have the same skill set as you is that you end up with an unbalanced and dysfunctional team.

I know a business owner who is quite introverted and despised aggressive people. As he built his management team, he surrounded himself with passive people who were all wonderful people but it wasn't in their nature to challenge the owner or each other on their opinions. Every time there was an issue to be dealt with everyone would sit on their hands until the owner gave his opinion and then agree with him even if they didn't agree or if they had a better solution. This often resulted in mediocre solutions that manifested into mediocre business performance.

On the other hand, I know of another business owner of a trades contracting company who had a dream management team. They all had varying talents and personalities with great ideas and insights to share. They constantly challenged the owner on issues and shared their ideas. Unfortunately, the owner didn't like to be challenged and would shut down the team often in an aggressive way. His typical response was, "I'm the boss, what I say goes". By not listening to his team he drove the company into many goal posts resulting in lower profits and disengaged employees who began putting in the minimum effort possible to get through the day. The best employees left.

An effective model to use when building a leadership team is to use DISC as I described in *Chapter 4, Know Your Communication DNA*. Each of the four styles offers its own attributes and value to a team which are explained below.

Director – This person tends to be the outgoing, task-oriented person. They will often be outspoken and will constantly push the team towards a decision and action. They are big picture people and don't like to get caught up in details.

Influencer – As the socialite on the team this member will provide a high energy, positive influence. They will be sure everyone gets along and break any tension that may build. They provide the team conscience by considering the human element of how decisions will affect people. Like the Director, they also prefer the big picture rather than details.

Steady Eddy – The stabilizing force. This person tends to be thoughtful and introspective. They need details before making decisions and if encouraged, they will ask questions and will get the rest of the team to take a deep breath before acting. They are team oriented and want to support the team anyway they can.

<u>Compliance Officer</u> – This person will get the team to plan, plan & plan. Also, very thoughtful, analytical and introspective they want all the details and contingency plans worked out before making decisions. This can often prevent the team from running into a goal post.

So how do you find the right balance on a team that not only has harmony but where team members will openly challenge you and each other to come up with the best solutions that drives your business toward your vision? The answer is to push outside your comfort zone and hire team members with personalities and skill sets that you do not have. A leadership team that doesn't possess all the attributes of the four styles risks being unbalanced and even dysfunctional. A team built with just Directors and Influencers will move forward quickly but will lack a plan and details causing them to make more mistakes. On the other hand, a team built with just Steady Eddies and Compliance Officers will have great plans and details worked out but may progress slowly as they get stuck by "paralysis through analysis".

Think of your team members as each being a piece of a puzzle with each piece being very different, but when they come together the result is a beautiful multi-dimensional picture. What is the makeup of your leadership team? Does your team have a balance of big picture thinkers and detailed oriented people or is it skewed too heavily with one style type? As the leader who understands everyone's communication DNA, use your knowledge to get the best out of each member of your team. If despite your best efforts, your team continues to be dysfunctional it might be time to rebalance your team by adding someone that possess the attributes that the team is missing.

The Role of the General Manager

I have mentioned the General Manager position several times in this chapter so let's clarify the role of this position. I have met with many blue-collar business owners who fill the role of the general manager in their business but don't really understand the role. The time they do spend in their office is usually spent fighting fires. Once the fires are put out, they look around trying to decide what to do next. After spending a few more minutes worrying about how they will make payroll they pick up their tools or hop on the forklift and start doing production work. It is their default position, where they are most comfortable. I can't tell you how many times I heard someone say, "If I'm not on the tools I don't feel like I'm working".

I invite you to look at random advertisements for general manager opportunities. You will find that the duties and responsibilities listed in the various ads are about eighty percent the same no matter the industry. That is because business is business and knowing how to manage a business is a transferable skill. In my own corporate career, I was a branch manager or regional manager in three different industries. In each case I was hired as the manager and was responsible for running a business unit that I had never worked in before. It took a few months to learn some of the ins and outs of that specific industry but once that was done, I was able to effectively manage the business because I spent my time working on all the items covered in this book. I wasn't a technical expert in that industry so I couldn't go on the tools even if I wanted to. I had no other choice but to work on the business and not in it.

To help you out I have provided a list of the most common duties and responsibilities of a general manager as shown in *Figure 13.2*. You will notice that most duties evolve around monitoring and ensuring tasks are getting done but there are no duties requiring the general manager to get on the tools or to do other lower value tasks them self. Do you spend most of your time working on the listed duties or do you spend your time working on the tools or other lower value tasks?

Fig 13.2

- ☑ Create action plans to achieve the company's long-term strategic plan
- ☑ Develop and monitor annual budgets
- ☑ Oversee all business operations to ensure that sales & profit goals are met
- ☑ Review financial statements and reports on a monthly basis and develop actions plans to improve business performance
- ☑ Continually look for opportunities to improve productivity and systems
- ☑ Manage Accounts Receivable to ensure positive cash flow
- ☑ Ensure that sales & marketing functions are executed to facilitate sales growth targets
- ☑ Maximize inventory turnover by monitoring and adjusting min/max levels
- ☑ Oversee HR functions including hiring, discipline, termination of employees and conflicts
- ☑ Conduct employee evaluations and approve wage increases
- ☑ Supervise and support the department managers to ensure productivity goals are met and safety protocols are followed and documented
- ☑ Resolve <u>escalated</u> customer service issues
- ☑ Approve purchase orders
- ☑ Oversee accounting functions to ensure best practices are followed
- ☑ Review and approve supplier/vendor invoices for payment
- ☑ Sign cheques & approve EFTs
- ☑ Delegate tasks and responsibilities to office and operations teams
- ☑ Ensure compliance of government regulations

Everything covered in this book is your responsibility as the General Manager. It is imperative that you spend at least eighty percent of your time working on your business and not in it. This means leading and developing your people with the highest level of skill, ensuring your marketing and sales programs are effective, continually looking for ways to improve efficiencies and profit, measuring performance of all departments and making the necessary adjustments, managing cash flow and reviewing your financial statements. All these areas represent a current or potential hole in your bucket. Your number one job as the general manager of your business is to continually look for ways to plug the holes in the leaky bucket. If you are successful, your bucket will overflow with profits and you will achieve the wealth and happiness you deserve.

About the Author

While growing up in Winnipeg, Manitoba, Tony fondly remembers the many family gatherings where he would listen to his parents and many aunts and uncles talk about faith, heritage and life's challenges. They were all blue-collar people who lead simple but happy lives. They laughed one minute and complained about the government the next. The one thing that was unshakable was their pride and values as honest, hardworking people.

With his blue-collar foundation of hard work ingrained, Tony aspired to a different life. He was born with a passion for business and the entrepreneurial spirit. He knew at a very young age that he wanted to be in business. Like many kids, he partnered with other kids in the neighborhood to run a lemonade stand. At twelve years old he "borrowed" his parent's lawnmower and went door to door looking for customers for his lawn cutting service. After cutting lawns he graduated to running a paper route where he and his brother would literally walk a mile in -30 deg F weather to pick up their papers and deliver them to customers as they walked home.

Upon graduating with a post-secondary education in business administration, Tony started his journey of learning business from hard knocks. After cutting his teeth in sales during the economic downturn in the early eighties he was promoted to sales manager at the age of twenty-five in the electronic security industry. He then became a branch manager at thirty years old and went on to hold titles of Regional Manager or Branch Manager in a few blue-collar industries throughout his career. As he changed companies and industries, he learned firsthand that "business is business". Every company had people to manage, processes to account for and expenses to track and control. These varied experiences taught him how to apply standard business principles to different industries and achieve results in as little as three months.

After a twenty-five-year career in the corporate world, Tony yearned to be self-employed, so he started a water purification business in his community and then a small distribution business selling a home maintenance product through major retailers in North America. Running his own business taught him very valuable lessons about business ownership. Like most business owners he faced challenges with cash flow, people problems and all the other forces that seem to work against businesses. After running his own businesses for several years, it became apparent that running a business on a day to day basis was not his passion. His real talents and passion were in analyzing, strategizing and helping others succeed.

After some research, Tony discovered the world of business coaching and took an intense training program with the *Professional Business Coaches Alliance (PBCA)* and became a *Certified Professional Business Coach.* He now has his dream job where he combines his hands-on business experience, business coach training and passion for working with hard working blue-collar business owners to help them run more profitable and valuable businesses that provides the lifestyle they deserve.

Tony is married to his wife Diane, has two grown children and five grandchildren. When not working he can be found volunteering in his community. He is a Past Assistant Governor with Rotary International and enjoys training Rotary club leadership teams to grow vibrant clubs so they can have a positive impact in their communities. He also enjoys cheering for his two favorite sport teams, the Winnipeg Jets and the Winnipeg Blue Bombers.

Tony invites you to contact him at <u>tony@empoweredbusiness.ca</u> if you would like to book a speaking engagement, arrange a personal call to talk about your business or to comment on this book.

Bibliography

Robson, Dan, Maple Leafs coach Babcock discusses coaching philosophy, Sportsnet.ca, 17/02/17, https://www.sportsnet.ca/hockey/nhl/maple-leafs-coach-babcock-discusses-coaching-philosophy/

https://www.alessiobresciani.com/foresight-strategy/51-mission-statement-examples-from-the-worlds-best-companies/

https://www.discprofile.com/what-is-disc/overview/, 28/04/19

Hall, Doug, JumpStart Your Business Brain, Cincinnati Ohio, Clerisy Press, 2018

Warrillow, John, Built to Sell, Penguin Group (USA) Inc., 2012

Gerber, Michael E., The E-Myth Revisited, HarperCollins Publishers, New York NY, 1995

Sinek, Simon, Leaders Eat Last, Penguin Random House LLC, New York NY, 2017

https://en.wikipedia.org/wiki/Tin_Men, May 9, 2019

https://en.wikipedia.org/wiki/Two-factor_theory, May 9, 2019